Professional
PRESENTATIONS

About the author

Shirley Hughes is an independent communications consultant, writer and partner in the successful training programme 'The Professional Presentation'. Formerly a senior client service director and associate director of the multinational advertising agency Lintas: Australia, presentations were an everyday event for Hughes. She brings a wealth of practical experience—and a sharp eye for the funny side of making presentations—to this commonsense guide to doing it well and enjoying it in the process.

Professional

PRESENTATIONS

A Practical Guide
to the Preparation and Performance of
Successful Business Presentations

SHIRLEY HUGHES

McGRAW-HILL BOOK COMPANY Sydney

New York   St Louis   San Francisco   Auckland   Bogotá
Caracas   Hamburg   Lisbon   London   Madrid   Mexico   Milan
Montreal   New Delhi   Oklahoma City   Paris   San Juan
São Paulo   Singapore   Tokyo   Toronto

**National Library of Australia
Cataloguing-in-Publication data:**

Hughes, Shirley.
  Professional presentations.
  ISBN 0 07 452727 4.
  I. Business presentations. I. Title.
658.452

Produced in Australia by McGraw-Hill Book Company Australia Pty Limited
  4 Barcoo Street, Roseville, NSW 2069
Typeset in Australia by Midland Typesetters Pty Ltd
Printed in Hong Kong by Dah Hua Printing Press Co. Ltd

Sponsoring Editor: Philip Alexander
Production Editors: Katie Wallace, Valerie Marlborough
Designer: Wing Ping Tong
Cartoonist: Yolande Bull

Contents

SECTION V Presentation planning

SECTION VI Presentation preparation

SECTION VII Presentation aftermath

Preface

This is a book about what is referred to in the world of business and administration as 'making presentations', professionally. This is how it came about.

Not so long ago, after many happy years in marketing and advertising, I was heading for the restful hills, savouring at last the prospect of time to have time. Time for pursuits and pleasures, for old friends and new ventures. Time for Tashkent on a one-way ticket, if the spirit moved me, or time to grab the golf clubs and blaze my way to the single-figure handicap in six months, tops!

There I was, dreaming of these imminent delights, when in marched a long-time and somewhat over-active client—not ready by a long shot for such indulgences himself, and not convinced that anyone else should be either.

'You can't go prancing off to God-knows-where just because you feel like it', he bellowed. 'Got things for you to do! Our young managers are bright as shiny buttons, but they can't make decent presentations in a pink fit! You know how to do it—you've done it for years— what about teaching them the ropes? Think about it. Call me!' And off he stomped, old habits, I noted, dying hard.

I did think about it. I remembered the time of being a young manager myself, when for all the lofty education and the proudly parental new briefcase, my early contributions to commerce were of a particularly low practical order.

Life on the learning curve was then (and still is) a dizzying experience. Facts must be mastered, names and functions understood, sales sheets decoded, and R&D demystified. And the day surely comes when your potty training is over and you are suddenly expected actually to manage something! Part of this awesome and exciting development is 'making presentations', professionally and often.

I saw, looking back down the long time-tunnel of trial and sometimes triumph, that making presentations has been and still is one of the least taught and most used of our business communication techniques.

The client had a good point. First came a training course, 'The Professional Presentation', trialled and tailored to improve the skills of managers in need. Now this book has followed, and if it helps just one soul struggle through early presentation days, or helps the somewhat more experienced get better at it, then keeping Tashkent on hold and my handicap in double figures will both have been worth the wait.

Observation of fellow-sufferers, experience, and more recently the training course itself, have taught me that the demons which plague most presenters fall into two broad categories which we can nickname 'Ego' and 'Info'.

'Ego' is the catch-all for everything to do with a presenter's personal performance. 'Info' describes all the myriad details of the organisation, planning and particularly the preparation for the great event—or the intellectual contribution, if you prefer.

For many presenters by far the most disturbing of the two is the dreaded 'Ego', the endless nagging concern about how they will perform on the day, how they will sound and look and feel, how they can even get through their presentation without throwing up or making some other kind of fool of themselves in the eyes of their audience.

For this reason, the problems and solutions of the 'Ego' demon are dealt with early in the sections which follow. Thereafter we can deal calmly and in detail with the 'Info' components of all well-structured presentations.

A word of encouragement. Very few of us are naturally gifted presenters, those who can see the track of their presentations so clearly and then deliver them with just the right style and emphasis. Such folk are very rare. The rest of us have to work at it.

But you can get there and I sincerely hope you do. Making good presentations—making them really professionally—is not only worthwhile, it can also be a lot of fun. When you learn to *like* making presentations, you will look forward to each one with pleasure, you'll be a top performer, and appreciation will surely follow.

I've enjoyed writing this book. I hope you, the reader, find it practical, useful and instructive. And if any of you would like to get in touch, well, for now the deep rough off any fairway should find me!

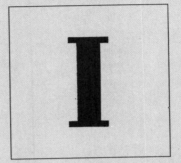

SECTION

I

Introduction

1

INTRODUCTION

The pain and the promise

Making presentations is and will continue to be a necessary evil and an everyday event for managers and administrators everywhere. We are constantly presenting ideas and information to each other—to our colleagues and customers, our advisers and suppliers, our boards and our staff—on every imaginable subject. Often we are seeking important decisions as a result.

Some presenters are well organised and highly articulate. More frequently, however, we make presentations so poorly that, in a world feeding voraciously on information and inspiration to fuel its progress, it sometimes seems a miracle that we ever managed to talk our way out of the cave!

Our audiences assemble with hope in their hearts. Invited, they come willingly to listen to us. Too often they depart deeply disappointed, confused at best and comatose at worst, with decisions unmade, opportunities lost, and respect at half-mast.

What goes wrong? Why is it that we torture ourselves so painfully when we have to make presentations? How do we manage to do it so badly, so often, and to waste so much time and energy in the process?

None of us sets out to make muddled, boring, stumbling and seemingly pointless presentations, overloaded with irrelevant information and unleashed on our long-suffering audiences like unguided missiles. We do the best we can, we think, and we have a perfect excuse for not doing it better.

Quite simply, most of us were not taught *how* to make a good presentation . . . how to think it through, how to plan it in every detail and then how to deliver it with clarity, persuasion and confidence.

Looking back to my early working days, it seemed to be airily assumed that no matter how inexperienced we were in life and in business, somehow we all knew how to do these wretched things called presentations. It was assumed that as we took our first, trembling step into the ranks of management, some magical mutation would occur and we would emerge, fully winged and tasselled, as brilliant presenters.

Hi, Moses, your visual aids were great!

If we were fortunate we might be exposed to a truly eloquent or passionate presenter early in our careers and perhaps learn something from that example. But what? Such folk can be so spell-binding to the uninitiated and inexperienced manager—viewing their dazzling presentation perhaps more as an observer than as an audience participant—that style could obscure craft. The secret of how they did it was not easily detected, leaving us to wrestle with the unanswered and troubling question: 'How can I *ever* be as good as X?'

Most of the time we were simply left to do the best we could and if we actually managed to bumble our way through a few presentations without dropping the charts or bumping into the furniture, then we were okay and well on our way to career mediocrity—encouraged only by the occasional and untruthful 'well done' floating in our wake and mindlessly relieved that it was all over for the day. Time and experience might add a little polish, but few possessed the key to unlock the door between competence and excellence.

For some, things are starting to improve. Special courses designed to upgrade the presentation skills of individuals are becoming available.

These are usually organised by larger corporations for small and deserving groups of mid-to-upper level managers, who have demonstrated their value and staying power. Enlightened and affluent companies recognise that improved presentation skills (better communication, if you like), must mean better business results.

Such presentation skills courses are expensive, however. Participation is closely confined to those with the firmest grasp on the corporate ladder and it's unlikely that large sums are ever going to be spent training highly mobile younger managers for the benefit of their next employers.

So, help has come for a small band of middle managers with stable employment habits—and perhaps they in turn can help their colleagues.

What of the rest? What of the managers in companies which do no training, what of administrators tucked away in uncaring councils or struggling in government instrumentalities? Above all, what of the legions of junior managers, for whom good habits learned young can stand them in good stead for all of their long careers? Who will help them through the pain of presentations?

This book will, and that's a promise. What follows can help you unravel the mysteries of preparing and making first-class professional presentations, regardless of your subject.

At first you will get a little better. Then, with growing understanding, discipline and practice, you'll get a lot better. One day (not too far away either), you can be simply terrific. You can be as confident, eloquent and persuasive as you choose to be. You can have that deep-down, good feeling that comes from knowing that you got it right— that you did something useful, and that you did it well. You will know that you have lost the pain forever and that you can live up to *your* promise of a bright career.

Promises, promises! Right now they may seem to be very large promises indeed.

'Piffle!', you cry. 'No one can help me! I get terribly nervous . . . my knees knock . . . my palms get sweaty . . . my tongue gets in a tangle . . . I'm terrified of the audience . . . petrified of making a fool of myself . . . and if anyone asks me a question I freeze—even though I remember later I knew the answer as well as my own name . . .!'

Ever felt that way? Even a little bit? I certainly did, once upon a time. I can still remember as vividly as yesterday, the silent anxiety of my first big presentation. It got done—heaven only knows how—but afterwards I couldn't remember a single word or the smallest detail of the discussion that followed. Mentally wiped out by the nervous tension, it was hours before I could bring myself to ask what had happened.

'Oh', came the reply, 'It went well—very useful—well done!', and a fat lot of learning or comfort I got from that response!

If you look back on the cry of anguish, you will see the first big barricade that stands between any would-be presenter and top communication. It's 'me-my-and-I' egomania all the way. Like a heavenly angel, you may indeed be the instrument of your message, but you are *not* its substance.

If you really want to be a good presenter, park your ego for the time being—put it in your briefcase, shove it in your handbag, or hide it in your Honda—at least while you read this book.

Don't worry! You can have it back later, all bright and shiny. In the meantime remember that ego can block the path to understanding more effectively than a barbed-wire fence—and with just about as many prickles.

It's time to stop thinking about yourself and to start thinking about others. The others whose help you may need in getting your presentation together . . . the others who may form part of your presentation . . . and above all, the others who will be your audience—what they are, who they are, what they need to know, and how you can help *them*.

Now, with ego tucked safely away, and thoughts of others uppermost in your mind, let us begin the serious business of turning you into an A-grade presenter.

Let us begin with the stunningly simple question: 'What on earth is a presentation anyway?'

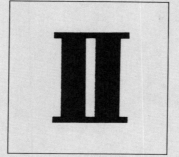

SECTION

II

What is a presentation?

1
Definitions

It seems to me a pretty useful notion to have some idea of what a presentation *is* before you try to do one.

Once you start looking for this simple truth you'll find that definitions abound. You can start with your colleagues. They'll have all sorts of ideas, but they may secretly be as mystified as you are and wouldn't dream of owning up to it. You can try the boss (after lunch is best) and hope for words of keen revelation. You can even tackle the dictionary and ponder the value of 'act of presenting, or state of being presented'. A big help, that is!

Perhaps you can think about what a presentation *isn't*. Thinking about what something isn't before deciding what it *is* can be a rather long-winded way of going about it, but it does have one big benefit. It can really help you unclutter your brain.

So, what is a presentation? Knowing what it is and what it is not—*knowing the difference*—will be a giant stride in starting to develop your skill as a presenter. Let us first see what a presentation is *not*.

2
A discussion

A discussion is almost always an informal event, and often takes place with little or no notice. We say to each other: 'Have you got a minute? I'd like to have a quick chat about such-and-such.' Or: 'Let's get the group together in ten minutes . . . we should discuss so-and-so and make sure we all know what we do next.'

Simple, straightforward and not in the least intimidating. There are exceptions, of course. If the chief executive tells you, 'Be in my office in five minutes. I want to discuss your future!', *that* can be a bit awesome. But generally we approach discussions quite cheerfully, without fear and with little preparation other than digging out the odd file or reference note.

In a discussion everyone is free to and indeed should participate. Of course, the discussion must have been arranged by *someone*. Let's

Discussions can be fun when everyone contributes . . .

call him the Leader, but he shouldn't take this handle too seriously. In the discussion, if the Leader starts getting too heavy and wants to talk all the time, then he's wasted the opportunity to hear the views of others. He should have stayed in his office and talked to his pot plant in the first place. The leadership role should always be very light in a discussion, otherwise the whole thing's a failure.

There should not be any silent, brooding listeners either—at least, not for the whole of the discussion. If you're part of a discussion, you're there because your opinion is sought and has value. Deep contemplation and zero contribution is a no no. You may well look like the in-house intellectual, but you'll be no fun in a discussion and you probably won't be asked again.

To a discussion, we bring our existing knowledge and views to share and explore with others on an informal basis. We're all more or less equal, the hierarchy's on hold and the good idea doesn't care who had it.

A discussion may very well *follow* a presentation, and frequently does—but if it breaks out in the middle of your presentation you can lose control and be in Big Trouble. More of this later. For now it is only necessary to grab the thought that a discussion is not and never will be a presentation.

3
A speech

Of course we *speak* when we make a presentation, but a speech as we generally understand it is a different form of communication altogether and serves quite different purposes.

A speech has a much more formal feel than a presentation. Scripts, lecterns, stages and microphones can come into play, often serving to separate speakers from their audience, and enhance their 'authority'.

In presentations, presenters and their audiences almost always have a common cause, mutual business interests. Speakers, however, need have absolutely nothing in common with their audiences. Speakers are the authorities on their subjects and the audiences are present out of interest, out of compulsion, or sometimes just to get out of the rain.

For example, given a bit of reading, research and preparation time, I could probably put together a speech on, say, 'The Doleful Social Consequences of the Changing Course of the Zambesi River'. You, as my audience need have absolutely no advance knowledge of this topic.

For whatever quaint reason, you come to hear my speech, and later you will depart a lot or a little wiser. Nonsense though this may seem, what is important is that you didn't need to know anything about the Zambesi beforehand, and *you don't need to do anything about it afterwards.* You simply attended an 'information' speech.

There are other kinds of speeches which, as we shall see, are not presentations either—by my definition.

There is the ever-popular 'goodwill and understanding' speech, much favoured by corporate heavies and other assorted leaders. These speeches are usually designed to give the troops a pat on the back for good deeds done well and to provide a passing glimpse of the Big Picture. As such they have a valuable purpose.

One great corporation with which I had a long and happy association does this better than most, and the chief executive's annual address to management is anticipated with considerable pleasure. Nicknamed years ago the 'Oh! Be Joyful', the title stuck. To their everlasting credit, the company sends out its invitations to attend 'The OBJ'—which are received with a smile and a chuckle, and everyone thoroughly looks

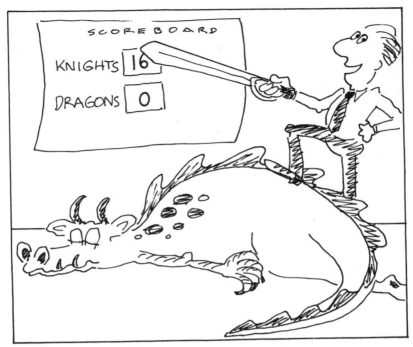

Our latest results have been quite spectacular

forward to the event. A tiny triumph for good PR, and a major recognition of the value of goodwill and understanding.

So the chief executive delivers the 'OBJ' speech, but no one is expected to take any action as a result—*no one has to do anything about it afterwards*—except, perhaps, feel good.

Then there is the 'entertainment' speech—of which the most shining example is the truly polished after-dinner version. The great performers of this genre are wondrous to behold. Alive with wit and style, they can reduce the crustiest group to laughter. They brighten our lives with the pleasure they give us, with the skill they display—and here again *we don't have to do anything about it afterwards*—except perhaps try to relate their anecdotes, as best we can.

In all of these kinds of speeches, the speaker is the authority and is in complete control of the event. The audience may very well mutter or fidget, eat and drink, laugh or cry, or simply nod agreement with the words of wisdom. Essentially, the speaker is in control and the audience is *passive*—and if any of 'em do get out of hand, we can always thrown them out!

An audience is not expected to arrive at any meaningful decision as a result of a speech—nor to agree to any precise course of action. These are not reasonable objectives for a speech.

This at last brings us to the thorny question of a presentation—what it is, how it works and who does what.

4
A presentation

Let me offer you a very simple definition. Let me suggest to you that:

A presentation takes place in order to persuade a mutual-interest audience to reach one or more decisions, or to agree to a course of action.

Once we accept that definition, then the whole process of preparing and delivering a presentation comes into focus. We actually intend to *achieve* something! To move events a tottering step forward.

A presentation is not an occasion for you to heave buckets of information over your audience, no matter how fascinating that information may be to you. If that's all you want to do, make a speech. Or preferably send a memo and don't waste everybody's time.

In a presentation you should use the precious time you have and the time and attention of your audience, to focus on *decision and action.*

Side by side with this definition comes the realisation that in order to structure your presentation (so that your audience will arrive at whatever decision or course of action you have in mind), you *must have an objective.*

Your working objective

Precisely, and well in advance, you must decide exactly what it is you want to achieve. Confusion certainly lies ahead for the presenter who fails to realise that preparation for a presentation begins with the simple question: 'What is the objective of my presentation?'

The answer to that question is the beginning of all the work you will then undertake to make sure that your presentation is clear and persuasive—that from beginning to end, you, your colleagues and your audience know exactly why they're there and what is expected of them.

Without an objective

Consider what happens when a presentation doesn't have a clear objective. Let's say we are the audience. We are made welcome, find our seats, exchange pleasantries with our chums and settle down with our coffee. Away goes the presenter. He or she has most of our attention but very seldom all of it. After all, we're only human and we have lots of other things to do and places to be.

The presentation meanders to an end. No one actually asks us directly to *do* anything and we depart in varying degrees of haste to our next encounters. 'Thank you so much', we say, out of ingrained politeness. 'We'll be in touch.'

Later, when we have a moment to catch our breath, we recall the presentation and a big bell clangs in our heads.

The presentation! What were we supposed to do next? Is the presenter going to contact us or should we have a meeting? Now if you have to have a meeting to decide what the presentation was about, what on earth was the point of the presentation in the first place! It might sound silly but it happens, time and time again. However, if your meeting's going to be about what you're going to do next, that's different. That's progress.

Back to the presentation—let's say it's a good one with a sharp, clear objective, and let's look more closely at who's doing what.

You and your audience

As the presenter, you're the Leader. You may well be the only presenter, or you may have decided that some points are better covered by one or more of your colleagues. Either way, you are in charge. Your role is very clear: you are the Leader and will be seen to be so. (Your leadership role is in sharp contrast to that in a discussion, where too strong a leader can swamp the event, as we have seen.)

The role of your audience is also clear. Unlike an audience attending a speech, they haven't just wandered in off the street. They've arrived in response to your invitation to attend a presentation on a subject of common interest to you both and they've come willingly. From your opening statement which confirms or announces the objective of your presentation, your audience will know that they, too, have come to do a job, not just to drink the coffee. They know that they're going to have to do something at the end of your presentation—and because of this they're going to be listening very closely indeed to what you have to say.

As the presenter not only is your leadership role clear, but you've got a lot of responsibilities to go with it. The chief of these is to *help* your audience—to help them arrive at their decision in favour of your objective. To accomplish this, when you are preparing your presentation you're going to have to sift through your treasure house of data and make quite sure that you select the right information and the right amount of it to support your proposal.

In so doing, keep in mind that you have absolutely no right to bore your audience witless! More often than not, inexperienced presenters want to reveal everything they ever knew of a topic, unaware of the likelihood that their audience either knows most of it anyway, or that it's irrelevant to their argument.

Quantity is not quality and if it's not relevant, dump it without a second glance. Sifting for relevant argument is, of course, easier said than done, but you'll get there, by thinking of your audience and always asking yourself, 'What do they know and what do they *need* to know in order to understand my proposal?'

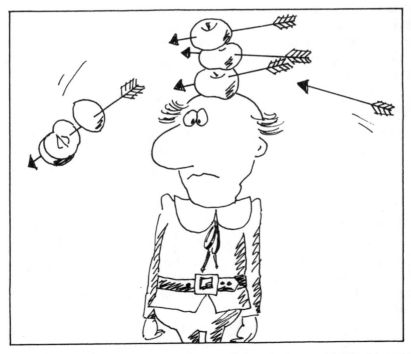

They *know* this apples trick, William . . . do we really have to show-and-tell like this again?

You have no right, either, ever to threaten your audience. That really *is* a mug's game—and you only have to think for one second about your own reaction to threat to know that you're on a loser here! If not accepting your proposal has a legitimate down-side, then deal with it honestly. Theatrical threat, perhaps, should be reserved until you begin your political career.

Finally, wise presenters make quite sure that their audiences feel the presentations were created specifically for them. They're not interested in to whom the presentation may have been made previously, what they said, or how wonderful they thought it all was. That's your business, not theirs. You can put all that in your collection of Golden Memories, but keep it out of *this* presentation.

A key to making great presentations is, as we mentioned in the previous chapter, forgetting about yourself and thinking of others . . . thinking of the value and relevance of your objective to the group you're presenting to . . . thinking of what they need to know in order to help them reach their decision . . . and treating your audience with consideration and courtesy in all things.

You will have legitimate self-interest, of course you will! That's what your presentation is all about. You want to get something changed, developed or decided, and with your clearly stated objective that will be no secret to anyone. But if you ever hope to persuade anyone to do anything, you have to see the proposal from the point of view of others. That's how it works.

In summary, then, what is a presentation? Nothing more or less than:

> *A pre-arranged, persuasive event, for which a realistic objective is clearly defined at the outset and for which careful and thorough preparation is undertaken to ensure you can successfully reach understanding and agreement.*

The human factor

For any presentation, good preparation is one thing, and performance is another thing altogether. They are the two quite separate aspects of any presentation. To a greater or lesser extent, we all have differing degrees of difficulty with one or the other, according to our own abilities.

Some of us are wonderfully clear thinkers—and gibbering idiots on our feet. Some are silver-tongued, born again snake oil salespeople—for whom performance holds no terror, but whose ability to thread complex and connected argument together is a touch suspect. For most of us, however, it's a bit of both, but there seems to be little doubt that performance, the Human Factor, causes us the greater anguish, particularly when we're new at the game.

We do our preparation for a presentation largely alone. We can think it through alone, we can quietly seek help and advice as we need it, but the moment inexorably arrives when we have to stand and deliver! Later we are going to look in detail at preparation for presentations, but let us first slay some of these performance dragons, so that we can move on with greater personal confidence. Let's have a look at some of these human factors that so unravel the unwary.

Presentation performance

5
Presentation behaviour

There are areas of presentation over which you have absolute control—areas of your personal performance—your style—which you will develop and polish for as long as there are presentations for you to make. These include how you feel, how you look, how you sound, and how you create the mood for your presentation. Simply put, how you behave.

Appropriate presentation behaviour is tricky. If you get it wrong you can feel very uncomfortable. What is worse, you may make your audience feel uneasy, even unwittingly embarrass or insult them. This can seriously damage your message and we don't want any of that!

Right now, chances are you'll be alright in some areas, but have bad habits in others. Don't we all? What we have to learn is to get all the behaviour areas right—and then make sure our behaviour is appropriate for each individual presentation. No two presentations are ever the same and what is right for one may be quite wrong for the next.

Consider: for some presentations we need to be quite formal and for others more relaxed. Some must be serious, others more cheerful. In some we need to move, in others we don't. In a small room all can hear a soft voice, but in a large room they cannot. These are just some of the different aspects of presentation behaviour and there are many others.

Let us deal, first, with the blight that afflicts so many presenters, regardless of their subject or the size of the occasion. Once and for all, let's help you deal with the dreaded 'nerves'.

6

Nervousness

You never *need* to be nervous during any presentation, providing you prepare for it thoroughly, and providing you hold on to one very simple thought:

Your audience is not your adversary!

Why on earth should they be, least of all in a presentation? They might come to a *meeting* for a punch-up, but they're not likely to arrive at a presentation with anything other than an open mind and a measure of curiosity. Otherwise they wouldn't have come in the first place. On the contrary, many will be actively looking forward to hearing what you have to say.

Many inexperienced presenters have an almost mindless fear of their audience. Yet you have only to think of *yourself* as a member of an audience and to recall your own feelings of anticipation, to realise how misplaced this fear really is.

Your audience has come to your presentation because you invited them, in the reasonable expectation that they're going to hear about useful ideas, profitable opportunities, answers to tough problems and good news. At worst, you may be outlining some bad news, but you'll be using this to make suggestions for correction. *That's* what a presentation is supposed to do, remember—not merely to supply information, but to propose action.

I guarantee that few if any members of an audience will ever arrive at your presentation smouldering with antagonism, spitefully ready to pounce on you at the slightest opportunity! Apart from any other considerations, such behaviour would be viewed by their colleagues as deeply anti-social and thoroughly bad form. After all, this is a business occasion, not all-in mud wrestling! So, what then do you really have to fear?

Questions? Certainly, you'll get questions. It's a peculiar presentation that doesn't and we'll be dealing with this issue later. For now, take it from me, you'll be able to handle the questions—for the very simple reason that it's *your* presentation. You prepared it, you're the expert, so chances are pretty good you'll know the answers.

If you're still a bit nervous, try this thought:

Preparation is your best defence.

Long before you have to make your presentation, you'll be preparing for it and in so doing you'll become the expert on your subject. *Then* you will rehearse your presentation. Rehearse it again and again, if that's what it takes to give you confidence and to add the polish. Here are some rehearsal ideas to get you going.

Rehearse on cassette

You know what you want to say, now say it. Grab the ghetto-blaster and your notes and put your presentation down on tape. Hear what it sounds like. Not what *you* sound like. You're thinking of your audience here, folks. Listen to your argument, not yourself. Is it clear? Does it flow well? Quite simply, does it make as much sense as you thought it did and as it should?

I've often used this rehearsal technique—and been appalled! Loads of long-winded rubbish and personal hobby-horses are horribly revealed on play back and out they go! On the other hand, sometimes a little gem appears, an almost ad-libbed thought with more insight and value than first realised and deserving more attention in revision.

That's what you do next. Revise. Straighten out your presentation, clean it up, make it work and then tape it again.

This time you can start to listen to yourself as well. Listen for your pace. Listen to the pauses and the emphasis. They should be there—after all, you don't want to drone all through your presentation in a monotone and put everyone to sleep!

Rehearse with colleagues

Consider asking some of your colleagues (preferably those with some knowledge of your subject) to hear you go through your presentation.

This can give you a good, commonsense filter. Your colleagues will come fresh to your ideas and should be able to spot any areas of loose thinking, or places for improvement. Of course, you have to let them say so! Don't waste their time helping you if you're not prepared to listen to their advice. You don't necessarily have to act on it—but you do have to listen. Seems a fair exchange to me.

Rehearse on video

This is a similar technique to cassette or colleague, but more revealing.

It has the added advantage of capturing any unfortunate gestures or other peculiarities that may be creeping into your presentation style. Few of us are ready to believe that we have any nasty habits, until the video reveals all!

One dear and talented man I worked with was a good presenter, wise and witty, and always perfectly prepared. On his feet, however, his posture was so odd that he always managed to look like a grovelling head waiter, bowing Madam Megabucks to the best table. Once we got him straightened up he was unbeatable.

A charming and intelligent research woman in our company often resembled a huddled and sinister soothsayer. We got her to sit up, offer the odd smile now and again and her sincerity readings went off the scale.

My worst habits were more physical, with arm-waving and karate chops at almost lethal levels. I didn't even know I was doing it and wouldn't have believed how distracting this could be until I saw it for myself on video. Clothes with pockets were a big help in sorting this one out!

Always make time for rehearsal

You'll live to regret it if you don't. Whichever way you decide to rehearse, make sure you do it. There is absolutely no substitute for rehearsal and absolutely no excuse for not doing it. If anyone ever says to you, 'Oh, you shouldn't rehearse—it takes away all the spontaneity!', you have my personal permission to thump them in the ear. That attitude is either dead lazy or just plain stupid—that kind of spontaneity you don't need.

So much for rehearsal. I think we've all got the point.

Don't panic

One final point on nervousness. Presenters' nerves can often be caused by the fear or fact of losing their place as they are rolling through their presentations.

For a split second they take their eye off their notes, are distracted by a sound or movement, or have a sudden lapse of concentration and panic sets in.

If you think about it carefully, there's no reason whatsoever that you need panic. You're prepared. You have your notes or agenda in front of you. All you have to do is pause. Just pause. It's perfectly okay to pause—it happens all the time. Your little pause, if it's noticed at all, will probably be taken as a tiny moment of contemplation.

Take a deep breath, gather your thoughts and move right along as though nothing happened, because for your audience, nothing did.

To a lost presenter a pause can feel like a lifetime, I know. But in the time it takes you to count to three slowly you can be back on the track and no one will ever know. So what if they do? Losing your place isn't a criminal offence. Any suspicion that you had become lost momentarily will be matched with sympathy. Don't forget, your audience are friendly, and it's happened to us all at some time or another.

Make your own space

Once again, don't forget that it's *your* presentation. Take your time before you begin. Take a couple of deep breaths and only begin when you're ready.

Then when you are ready, move into your presentation at your own speed and at the speed that's right for your subject and your material. Just because other people use different speeds, it doesn't mean you have to use theirs. Use yours.

Stand if it's right, or sit if you feel that's more appropriate to your audience. Do both if you choose. Move about if you want to. There are no fixed rules, but one word of warning—too much meandering can prove most distracting.

The important point is that you make your own space, and move at your own pace. You want to be as good as you can, but you must always be yourself. Being yourself, not trying to be someone else, will give you a good, tight grip on your nerves. After all, you'll know exactly who you're dealing with!

To calm the nerves

These are the best nerve-pacifiers I can think of and, if you always remember them, I know they'll work for you:

- Don't be afraid of your audience. They're really on your side.
- Preparation will make you the expert—so what have you got to fear?
- Always make time to rehearse, and rehearse thoroughly.
- When in doubt, don't panic!

Follow these rules and that should be the end of your nervous troubles.

The good news nerves

It's also worth considering that nerves can be good news, too. Getting a bit edgy before your presentation is very common and signals that your adrenalin is on the way up for the big event.

These pre-presentation nerves affect us all in different ways. I was inclined to get the thousand yard stare and prowl a lot, with the result that I'd sometimes trip over small objects in my path or unnerve a passing stranger with a mad, unseeing glare.

Pre-presentation nerves—live with them and be grateful—can give your presentation more zip than a fistful of multi-vitamins!

7
Moving well

This is a do's and don'ts department for you to think about—very seriously, I hope. Sadly, many presenters never even bother to think about their physical actions at all, never even realise that they can consciously plan and control the way they move in a presentation, just as effectively as they plan their content.

'Why should I?' you rightly ask. Quite simply, when you *do* you can enhance your message. When you *don't* you can make a big, unexpected mess of it and your careful content preparation goes down the tube! If you're not careful, careless movements can disrupt the attention of your audience, even distort the sincerity of your presentation. Let me give you a couple of examples.

The casual trap

A smart young client of mine, a product manager, was presenting her brand relaunch plans to her company sales conference. The atmosphere was receptive, interested, friendly and casual—and that's where she made her big mistake! She had a serious presentation to make and her preparation was spot on, but she wrecked the whole thing by over-playing casual and making the wrong moves.

Chummy as the girl next door, she perched herself on the edge of a table with one foot planted firmly on the floor—and proceeded to swing the other foot back and forth with a mesmeric rhythm. Very quickly the attention of her audience became glued to the flying Reebok and most of her message was lost. She had failed to realise that her serious purpose should have been reflected in more serious posture and the unconscious (and probably nervous) pendulum motion of her hoof had all but destroyed her presentation. A classic case of foot and mouth disease!

The grand gesture trap

A famous medical television personality—who now knows better— once became so involved in his subject he forgot about his hands. Talking about really serious matters—literally health and life, disease

29

and death—he became so concerned, so animated, that he started to whirl his wondrous long hands and didn't realise he was doing it. Every time he wanted to emphasise a point, which was frequently, he'd flap away in a most disconcerting fashion. The result was that he appeared theatrical and insincere, and much of the value of his information was wasted. His gestures were quite natural to him, but were unacceptable to his viewing audience.

Make no mistake! I'm all for gestures—the right ones in the right place at the right time, but they're a yawning trap if you get them wrong. If you're still not convinced, watch other presenters and you'll find it's great fun to spot even the everyday, distracting sillies.

The fiddling trap

Messing with clothing is popular. Pockets are endlessly explored, with contents that jingle, jangle, jingle. Ties are checked and straightened as though being worn for the very first time and belts are hitched with all the solemn purpose of Bulgarian weight-lifters confronting world records.

Objects can be a right menace, too. Pen arrangements, clusterings, are a favourite, with pen tapping sometimes raised to manic levels. Small calculators appear, to be moved lovingly back and forth as though to comfort the presenter by their very presence. Slide-changers are fondled and whirled, their leads painfully subjected to tests of strength and length and loyalty.

The worst of all, the prize terror of presentations, is unquestionably the telescopic pointer. Once in our grasp, we cannot seem to put them down! Long after they have served a useful purpose, in and out they slide, unconsciously betraying who knows what repression, to the growing distraction of desperate audiences and often to the dismay of suddenly aware presenters.

Gentle friends, where objects are concerned, *leave them alone*. Put them down. When you need them, use them. Otherwise, keep your hands to yourself!

Silent communication

If you have any lingering doubt about the effect of posture, gesture and motion on communication, there's a simple test you can do. Turn on your television set and turn off the sound. Pick a movie you haven't seen, or an episode of a series you don't usually view. Watch it for a while and tell me you can't follow what goes on! I think you'll find you can read pain and pleasure, contemplation and concern, love and laughter, and much more subtle reactions as clear as day, and with almost as much understanding of plot as you could achieve with sound.

This is the actors' gift, this ability to communicate meaning and nuance through movement. Every time you make a presentation, you too must bring a little of the actors' skill to the event. The better you learn to do so, the better your results will be.

Self-control

There's another kind of performer well worth a quick look—the really top poker player. In contrast to actors (and presenters), who are trying to *add* to communication through posture, gesture and motion, high-stakes poker players are trying to *suppress* any give-away signals.

Imagine, if you will, the degree of skill and self-control it must take to disguise strong emotions—disappointment, anger, joy, greed,

Mother!

delight—and how difficult it must be to handle the physical evidence of excitement, depression or fatigue.

Not for these high rollers the extrovert expression of posture, gesture and motion—unless they wish to lay false trails! There'll be times when, as a presenter, you too may need a poker player's control and discipline to disguise your true feelings. These possibilities will not occur to you until you learn to *think* about them. Hard.

In summary:

Posture

Standing or sitting, please don't slouch. Aside from the fact that it's disrespectful to your audience, it can easily give the impression that you don't really give a damn about your presentation. Granted, not all of us are blessed with a naturally elegant, reasonably upright posture, but we can all try.

I often think that people get into a bigger mess sitting down than standing up. Depending somewhat on the furniture, we manage to wallow and wriggle, elevate our knobbly knees, curl into the protective pre-natal position, and generally test our design specifications to their limits. Sometimes we sit too stiffly, puppeting falsely to various members of the audience as we address them.

Easy does it, folks! The right style, the right mixture of relaxation and respect and the type of improvement needed will be different for every one of you. But you'll never be as good as you *can* be if you don't consciously think about it and then find what's right for you.

Gestures

Use them, please. They brighten and punctuate any presentation if you use them well. Beware of exaggerated gestures which do not fit your meaning or which can confuse your audience. By all means, borrow from others. We all endlessly copy each other's gestures. If you do, make quite sure they fit—both you and your topic.

Above all, beware of the distracting gestures that are unconnected to your presentation. Head scratching and back stretching are personal indulgences we can all do without and your presentations will be all the better for their absence.

Motion

Finally, if you want to move, do it because you *planned* it. Do not suddenly break into a trot as the spirit moves you!

Avoid treasure hunting. If you have things to reveal, items to demonstrate, goodies to fetch, you must know in advance exactly where they are and how to get at them. Have them handy—or have them placed away from your presentation position if you want to add dramatic effect by moving to get them. Don't expect it to be okay if you haven't thought about it in advance and planned exactly how and when you intend to move.

Why all this fuss and bother about posture, gestures and movement? For the very simple reason that *you are your own best visual aid.* You owe it not only to your audience but to yourself to be as good as you can possibly be. With thought, watchfulness and practice you're going to make it.

8
Let the eyes have it

Have you ever realised how much comment and advice is elicited by our eyes?

In our childhood we receive doting approval. 'Oh, hasn't little darling got *beautiful* eyes!' we hear. Later, this is followed by the admonition, 'Don't stare! It's rude'. Usually there is scant explanation why one's lovely optics shouldn't be used for the intended purpose, and confusion sets in early in life.

Having grasped the don't-stare-it's-rude rule, life proceeds down the path of learning and mischief to the inevitable collision with Authority. Large and cross, it cries, '*Look* at me when I'm talking to you!' Have you ever tried to do that without staring?

So we stumble on, our orbal antics ranging from 'wide-eyed innocence' to 'eyeball to eyeball' confrontation. Is it any wonder we may have grown a bit shifty by the time we have to face the real world?

Poets speak of the eyes as 'the windows of the soul', and perhaps it is so. Long ago I heard an admiring description (of a bright and helpful friend) that I have never forgotten and often borrowed since. 'I really *like* that chap', said our mutual acquaintance, 'The light's on and somebody's home!' That's the impression you too can create when you learn to set aside your shyness and let your genuine enthusiasm shine through your eyes.

The audience ignored

How often have you attended a presentation, listened attentively, seen everything that took place and yet come away with the feeling that somehow you hadn't really participated in the occasion—that something was missing.

It was! The presenters never once took the trouble to look at *you*. They looked at their notes. They looked at their props, their papers and visual aids. They studied the walls and the ceiling. But they never once looked you in the eye—to recognise your presence and to acknowledge your value. Discourteous though that was, it's a great example to learn by.

There's no excuse for such disregard of individuals in an audience but there is an explanation. Presenters are tense, anxious to get going, and have a lot of territory to cover. They have things on their minds. Unfortunately the audience isn't always one of them. In all the excitement they forget the golden rule—thinking of others, not only of themselves. You're not going to forget, are you?

Bulls-eye cures

If you are secretly uncomfortable about looking people in the eye, here are some hints to get you over your problem, to help you make your audiences feel as welcome and involved as they have every right to be:

- First, practise looking at everyone with whom you come into daily contact, really looking at them, making real eye contact, not just skidding by. Look at your friends, family, the people who serve you, your colleagues, your customers if you have them.

. . . but it's more comfortable this way . . .

I'll be very surprised if they don't all feel how friendly you are all of a sudden!

- While you're at it, practise letting your eyes *react*. After all, you've got nothing to gain by going through life like a flat-eyed lizard! Let your eyes really show your interest, your amusement, your concern. It might feel a bit odd at first, but it'll be second nature in no time—when you find it doesn't actually hurt.

- Now that your eyes have lost their blank and shifty habits, you're ready for your presentation audience. You have to make a very conscious effort to look at every single individual, one at a time, as you go through your presentation, and you must train yourself to do this naturally.

- To be natural you should avoid bouncing left to right or right to left, working yourself into a too regular and sometimes inescapable rhythm. Instead, look first to one side and then to the other, sometimes moving directly from one person to their neighbour, but not always.

- Be very careful not to ignore the people seated closest to you. It's easy to do. Sometimes they'll be as close by as dinner companions and darting the eyeball in their direction won't do it. You may have to turn towards them too.

- The content of your presentation is also there to help you. Some of your points will be of more specific importance to one member of your audience than to the others, so address that point to that individual. If it helps to remind you, jot names in the margins of your notes, and when the time comes seek out those individuals in your audience.

- If your audience is too large to deal with one by one, visually divide it into small sections and then make sure you cover each one just as you would individuals. Very large groups would be rare for presentations but segmenting is also a handy technique to use for speeches, if you ever have to make them.

I don't like the word technique. It has too calculating a ring for my taste and has little place in the discussion of the courteous recognition of others. In the end, isn't that just plain good manners?

9
Let's hear all about it

In the unlikely event that you are trussed, tied and blindfolded, never fear! You're still in business. You still have your *voice*—the big bassoon of presentations.

What an instrument it is! Rather, what an instrument it can be, when you've learned to use it well, when you've mastered your control panel. Let's have a look at the options you have at your command.

Volume control

Like all your other presentation skills, you'll need to become accustomed to your volume control and really practice with it for best results.

Quite plainly, you do not want to create sonic booms in small rooms, nor to whisper in large ones. That's common sense. Everyone wants to be able to hear you and you want that too.

Small spaces and small audiences present no serious volume problems, but larger ones can be ticklish.

For a medium-sized or larger group it's as well to know that all those nice, warm bodies are going to soak up some of your sound. So, if you have rehearsed your presentation in your venue, decided to use or not to use a mike and your volume was fine, do remember to come up a notch when your audience assembles.

If you don't you may get off to one of those truly awful starts that goes, 'Good morning ladies and gen . . . What's that? You can't hear me? Is that better? Can you hear me now? Can you hear me at the back of the room? Right! Now, where was I . . .?'

Where you are is in a big mess, and you're off to an untidy beginning. You neglected to speak strongly enough and clearly enough to get everybody's attention from word one. Once again you've forgotten to think of others!

By the way, if the naturally light volume of your voice combined with the size of your audience and the size of the room *do* indicate that a microphone is necessary, then use one. But for goodness sake, set it up, blow in it, beat it on the head—do whatever you must to check it out *before* your audience arrives. Then just walk up to it and start. That looks and is thoroughly professional—and your audience is spared the searing pain of the electronic whiz-bangs, or proof that you can count.

Think about the possibilities of using your volume control *during* your presentation. Turn the volume up for all kinds of emphasis— dramatic point, surprise, alarm and excitement. Alternatively, many experienced presenters will actually turn the volume down when making a key point. This has the effect of forcing the audience to listen even more carefully than they might otherwise have done.

Try turning the volume up and down during your presentations and you'll find you can add subtle, dramatic emphasis to your message if it's necessary.

Speed control

It's perfectly okay, even desirable, to vary the speed of your delivery where it is appropriate to do so. After all, in our everyday speech we all do it all the time, without even realising it.

For example, faster speeds usually indicate our excitement or enthusiasm. Slower speeds can signal careful thought, as though we are reaching for exactly the right words to describe a matter of significance.

These speed variations are so natural to us all, their use in a presentation will be accepted without question—and they do give you the opportunity to add further colour and variation to your material.

Tone control

Bet you didn't know you had one! Well, you do, and so do the rest of us, and like the Speed Control we use it without thinking. Listen to those around you. Happy events we describe to each other in a higher, lighter tone than we use for the serious.

Once you can hear this for yourself, then you can learn to use it to help lift or shade your communication, to add further style and mood to your proposals.

The fine tuner

This is your mumble meter! This is the final tuning you must learn to give to the *sound* of your presentations. Mumbling is no good and must go.

In the end, it doesn't matter how well prepared your presentation may be if your audience can't hear you and cannot feel the enthusiasm, or reason, or conviction in your voice. If these sounds are missing, so too is a vital element of your presentation.

Until you can learn to use your voice effectively, to vary your volume, your speed and tone controls at the right moments and to fine-tune for clarity, it's time to head for the tool shed, the middle of the paddock, the bathroom—wherever you feel least inhibited—and let her rip!

Test your controls on something you know well. Epic poems and heroic bits of the Bard are very handy, if you can remember them. Telephone numbers will do just as well if you can't. For your practice, *what* you say doesn't matter. *How* you say it does.

In no time at all your voice will be rich and free—free to be heard clearly. You will have come to know your own voice. You will have mastered the main instrument of your presentations and, no doubt to their considerable relief, the family can have the bathroom back!

. . . ask not what your country can do for you, but what you can do for your country

10
Personal styling: the dress code

Like it or not, what we wear and how we wear it sends out signals about ourselves and our attitudes to others. What you wear in your own time is your own business. What you wear to your presentation matters.

Before you reach for the rags, there are three distinct elements to be considered in any presentation—your audience, your material and yourself.

Your audience

When you make a business presentation, do it in every sense of the word. Flamboyant or casual clothing is always inappropriate to business occasions and often downright disturbing to those in your audience with serious business decisions to make.

You may have the best idea since sliced bread, but if it's being proposed by a rumpled creature in bangles and beads, you're making it a bit tough for yourself. If your audience is conservative they're likely to be suspicious of *you* and that suspicion is going to rub off on their perception of your idea.

Of course, there will always be exceptions. If you happen to be a certified genius with the world pounding a path to your door, you can probably make your presentation in a bedsheet and get away with it. But if you're anything less, then watch it!

Get into the habit of reviewing your audience carefully, before every presentation. Ask yourself: who's attending, what kind of people are they and what kind of clothing is appropriate to *their* social attitudes and to the decisions you want to persuade them to reach.

Once in a while you may decide to surprise. If you do, be very careful and, in my opinion, when in doubt don't! A colleague and I once decided to fancy-dress for the presentation of a circus-based creative idea, in the misguided belief that our finery would be 'fun' and would add a whimsical touch to the occasion. It did that—but we looked and felt ridiculous when the time came to discuss serious matters at the end of our presentation. Our guests showed an under-

Oh! You're one of *those* angels!

standable reluctance to trust their futures to a couple of clowns! Wouldn't you?

The less your clothing has to say, the better you will be heard. The better your grooming, the more it will quietly emphasise your care and consideration.

Your material

If your presentation requires you to display charts or other visuals, or to demonstrate products, beware of clothing which clashes with their colours or messages.

You can colour co-ordinate with these goodies if you think it will help, but do not overwhelm them.

If you have to reach or stretch or bend for whatever reason, make sure that what you're planning to wear will be able to handle these manoeuvres as well as you can. Escapee beer-bellies are not a pretty sight. Yards of comely thigh may have their place in the scheme of things but not in your presentation.

The presentation of yourself

The personal styling and grooming of managers has come a long way since the hairy '60s and the slap-happy '70s and the new breed are looking smarter, more confident and more assured than they have for decades. They do not look as though they slept in their clothes. They look to have serious purpose.

So they do. The stakes are higher than ever before and the competition for personal recognition and promotion borders on ferocious. Call it the rat race if you will, with a slight curling of the upper lip, but the fact remains that given equal ability, it is often the little things that distinguish one contender from the next when it comes to the question of the next appointment, the juicy job. Good personal presentation is no small thing. It counts, for yourself and for your presentations.

Correct business attire affects both the wearer and the viewer. It provides a clear and accurate barometer of your own self-esteem and a reflection of your respect for your audience, and it will be recognised as such.

Aside from competitive considerations, I believe that being dressed comfortably is the most desirable condition in which to make any presentation. Not comfortable–sloppy, but comfortable–smart. Understated, well-cut, crush-proof and thoroughly comfortable. If you are comfortable, then you can get on with your presentation without giving your appearance a second thought and with your attention focussed entirely on what you have set out to achieve.

11
Setting the mood

Your presentation will always take place in one of two circumstances. Either you will set up the venue in advance and your *audience* will arrive or your audience will already be assembled and *you* will arrive. (Dead heats are extremely rare, create immense confusion, and should be avoided like the plague.)

In the first instance, when you have the benefit of an arriving group, setting the mood for the occasion is entirely in your hands and so presents no problems. You are in control from the start.

In the second case, however, you may have the odd mood problem to deal with before you begin and with Apache cunning you must learn to read signs. Some signs, of course, are unmistakable.

Reading the mood-signs

If the audience is chortling away as you arrive, having a thoroughly jolly time, then the mood is already cheerful. Once you have the undivided attention of your audience, you are ready to begin your presentation in an atmosphere which is relaxed and friendly. What happens next depends entirely on your subject and your behaviour.

On the other hand, you will sometimes arrive to find evidence of blood on the floor, your audience grizzling, glum and clearly at odds with each other. Why this niggling atmosphere exists is neither your business nor your fault. Whatever took place before your arrival was beyond your control and it is important to keep that in mind. It is, however, your responsibility to change the mood for your presentation.

Whether you do this with the crispness of your business-like readiness, with pleasantry or anecdote, or with the time-honoured, 'It will take me a moment or two to set up—would anyone like to take a break before we begin?'—it's up to you. How you handle it will depend on the circumstances and the size of your audience, but handle it you must in order to break the mood of misery and create the right atmosphere for your presentation.

Having taken a moment to read the signs and to accept or adjust the mood of your audience, you are ready to begin. Controlling the

... let Spot go first to see if they're happy!

mood is now over to you. You're prepared, rehearsed and ready—ready to relax and enjoy making your own presentation with skill and enthusiasm.

Don't panic if you don't seem to have the devoted attention of every member of your audience right from the start. With a good, clear objective and a well-crafted presentation, you're going to pick up any stragglers as you go. Remember, you're there to present ideas to their advantage and only a real dunderhead is going to miss the point. Your enthusiasm for your subject is going to play a large part in creating and sustaining the positive mood of your presentation and in involving everyone present.

Mood and enthusiasm

If you are doubtful that genuine enthusiasm can be as infectious as measles, let me give you just one example.

We were putting together a team presentation for a new account for our agency. In working up to this event we'd all become very involved in the project and genuinely interested in the product. Our advertising ideas were fair but at that time, frankly, not great.

The presentation day arrived and we'd been allocated one hour to pitch for the business, when the managing director of the potential client rather gruffly announced, 'I've got twenty minutes', ostentatiously cuffing his Rolex and busting the time contract wide open! His more junior colleagues, however, nervously said they could stay for the full hour and on that wobbly note off we went.

Something happened. Through one agenda point after another the enthusiasm we had built up for the product and its future began to shine through for all to share. In themselves, the so-so advertising ideas became irrelevant to the chemistry of the meeting and we all knew we would get them right later.

The managing director stayed for the full presentation, stayed for lunch, postponed his afternoon appointments to talk the project through and the next day we had the account. With booming sales and multiple awards for advertising excellence, that business partnership—born of little more than pure enthusiasm—has grown and prospered to this day.

Whether excitement is the mood you want, or cool business logic, or sympathy and understanding—whether you are offering creative ideas, detailing financial results, or reviewing social injustice—the way you do it and the mood you establish for your presentation is entirely in your hands. And it is important. It will have a profound effect on the way your audience receives your presentation.

12
Being yourself

If it should seem to you that controlling your nervous tension, consciously moving well, touching people with your eyes and wooing them with your voice, dressing to suit and modifying the mood of every presentation is beyond you or is perhaps a job for a first class phoney, you're wrong, on both counts.

They are merely the means to an end—making better presentations. They are the simple good manners of making your audiences feel more comfortable.

Only the incurably arrogant will decide that there is absolutely no room for improvement in their personal style and their presentation behaviour. For most of us, just thinking about these matters will, in itself, create improvement. The rest is up to you. How much improvement is needed only you can judge.

Making improvement in your presentation behaviour does not mean that you will suddenly, or even gradually, become one of thousands of cloned and interchangeable presenters. On the contrary, when you are no longer apprehensive and uncomfortable about making presentations, when you have mastered the art of good presentation behaviour, you will think less about yourself and more about your task.

You will know that the time has come to put aside the clichés of business language and mannerisms, to leave behind the over-eager business postures that reveal so much and mean so little. You will be free to concentrate on your message and your audience. You will be free to be the best of your natural self. You will become valued and well regarded—a credit to yourself and an asset to your organisation.

13
Considering your audience

Now we must move from thinking of you to thinking of the other human factor—your audience. Before you begin the preparation of any presentation, there are three important, basic questions you must always ask yourself about your audience:

- What do you know about **them**?
- What do they know about **you**?
- What do they know about your **subject**?

Your first answers to these questions will often be more questions, as we shall see. The ultimate answers will give you vital clues to guide you in the construction of your presentation and often the manner in which you will deliver it.

If you fail to consider your audience in advance, all kinds of nasties can befall you—ranging from the shock of greeting a bunch of strangers you suddenly realise you know absolutely nothing about, to the mid-presentation realisation that you're offering a great idea to a group which cannot act on your proposal. These are not recipes for successful presentations.

There is no such thing as not having time to do your audience review. Quite simply, it's a must. With practice, you will find it need not take you more than a few minutes, particularly if you are planning a presentation for a known group. Here too, however, take warning!

Assume nothing, and check everything—even if you *think* you know. People, circumstances and responsibilities change in the blink of an eye, the flash of a memo.

How silly are you going to feel when your chief departing guest thanks you warmly for your presentation and adds, 'By the way, I was reassigned last month and I'm moving on Monday. Very interesting presentation, though. Perhaps you'd like to talk to Charlie about it. He's my replacement. Did you invite him . . .?'

Knowing full well that you didn't and fighting back expletives, your day is now in ruins. Whose fault is that? Yours. You didn't review your audience, you didn't check, and you've just wasted hours of precious time and megawatts of energy talking to the wrong person. Which leads us to the first of our review questions:

What do you know about them?

Your first consideration is: who is attending your presentation. Not which group, but *who*. Never think of your audience in bulk terms, but as people. They are not the Staff, the Board, the Department, the Management, the Client, or any other collective. They are all individuals, each with different attitudes, needs, knowledge, expertise and responsibilities.

Your next most important consideration is your review of these individuals, to assess who amongst them can make a decision as a result of your presentation. If the answer to that is none of them, you're on a loser here. You're either planning to talk to the wrong people, or your presentation objective is unrealistic. See how it works?

Let's say that you know your decision-makers will be present and your objective is achieveable. Who else should be there? Others will also be affected by the decision, or 'will influence it and you need to be sure that these people are also present—certainly if *you* are issuing the invitations. Failure to invite them will be taken for what

... does that pair look familiar to you?

it is—callous disregard of their value to their departments or their company—and some will have very long memories indeed.

A third group should also be considered: those who will neither decide nor influence, but whose attendance may add to their knowledge. If in doubt, settle this with a quick call to your opposite number, with the straightforward question: 'I'm planning to invite A, B and C to our presentation—is there anyone else who should be included?' This is both simple courtesy and common sense—after all, if Charlie is now overlooked, it's not your fault!

Now that you know who, it's time to consider *what*, a string of further questions you will have to resolve. Here are some to get you thinking. Others you will develop for yourselves as you become more experienced. So, for each of the members of your audience:

- What do they know and what do they need to know in order to understand your presentation?
- What are their likes/dislikes in presentation style and format, if any?
- What are their attitudes to time, that is, length of presentation, time of day?
- What are they likely to do—will they respond immediately, or after consideration?

A keen observer once remarked that we humans will go to almost any lengths to avoid the pain of thinking, but thinking will get you the answers to these questions. So will checking, if you are not sure. Your presentation will be better prepared, more relevant and more persuasive from the moment you adopt the practice of reviewing your audience in detail, through questions.

What do they know about you?

If this seems a little puzzling, keep calm! It's quite simple, but does need serious consideration. First of all, for 'you', read first your company and then yourself.

It shouldn't be too difficult to make at least some assessment of what your intended audience knows about your company. They either know your company or they do not.

If they do, then they may consider you anywhere in the range between the best and kindest thing since Bambi, or the biggest bunch of bandits since The Wild Bunch hit the road. Whatever your conclusion, it will give you a feeling for the necessary tone and style of your presentation and some view of the manner in which your presentation will be received—whether you are entitled to expect a genuinely interested reception, or whether simply being believed will be one of your important presentation tasks.

If your audience doesn't know your company at all, this clearly suggests the need to establish your credentials—either before your presentation, or as an introduction to it. After all, we all need to know who's giving us advice.

Either way, the action you take will arise from the answer to your question, 'What does my audience know about my company?' If you can't find the answer from within your own experience, don't hesitate to ask around. You may get some valuable and unexpected replies.

Now, what does your intended audience know about you personally? If they don't know you at all, you will have to arrange to be introduced at your presentation or you will have to introduce yourself. This must be done properly. The manner in which you are introduced has considerable bearing on how your advice is going to be received.

If all or most of the members of your audience do know you, then how do they feel about you? How good is your working relation-ship? Do they trust you? Do they usually believe you? Are they likely to be receptive to a proposal from you on *this* subject? Or is there some groundwork to do?

Keep in mind that reviewing an audience which knows you should not be turned into an episode of either self-congratulation or neurosis and despair. All you have to assess is whether they know you and respect you, or whether you have to lift your game. If so, how and by how much, in order to make your presentation effective.

Internal company or departmental presentations can sometimes appear more daunting than the external variety. Often we have quite different attitudes, more personal prejudices, towards our colleagues, born of our day-to-day contacts with each other, than we do towards relative strangers. Nonetheless, the same analytical process must apply; the same questions are valid. Every internal presentation should be approached with as much care and preparation as for an external event.

The language trap

For an internal presentation it is likely that you will use the language and terminology which is familiar and understood within your department or organisation—in-talk, if you like.

If you are planning to make a presentation on the same subject to an external group then, as your mother used to say, watch your language! What was crystal clear to your colleagues may be as obscure as Swahili to the uninitiated.

Modifying your language for each separate presentation will not always be necessary, but often it will. You will always communicate more clearly if you use terms which are comprehensible to your audience, rather than simply slick and convenient for yourself.

So, use of language is another item for the audience review check list you will build up over time.

There's no detail of your presentation which you shouldn't check against your knowledge of the members of your audience. When you learn to do this well, the results will be evident in the quality of every presentation you make—and when you then come to ask yourself what the audience knows about you, you will be satisfied with the answer.

What do they know about your subject?

The answer to this question will give you the guidelines you need in order to plan the content of your presentation. Answers will range from nothing to a lot, and sometimes your audience will know even more about your subject than you do.

When your audience knows nothing or very little of your subject, you've obviously got some explaining to do. You will have to select the right background information and the right amount of it, in order to place your proposal in context.

For a well-informed audience, however, it is obviously quite different. You will either need no background at all, or just the briefest of summaries, which, incidentally, should be thought out with just as much care as for an uninformed audience.

The contrast between the two is really rather like the difference between teaching someone to drive, and teaching a driver to drive well. In the first instance you have to show the driver where the keyhole is. In the latter he knows that very well, and will be hurtling down the highway while you're still closing the door. The former needs to know about the keyhole. The latter's off and running, and any minute now is going to get cross because you're being a bore and wasting his time. He knows very well how to drive his BMW— he wants you to show him how not to bingle it!

So, you must assess the extent of your audience's knowledge of your subject before you can even begin to design your presentation.

Then you can plan it confidently, knowing that you'll be pitching it at just the right angle, just the right speed instead of heading off into the perilous murk of a no-think fog bank.

Now we know what a presentation is and now that we've explored the human factors as intimately as we can, given that you're out there and I'm over here, we are ready to begin the great adventure. We are ready to begin the detailed Organisation, Planning and Preparation of your presentation.

Presentation organisation

14
Bringing order to chaos

The sole purpose of good presentation organisation is to bring order to chaos and as a result ensure that you and everything you need will be ready when it should be—ahead of time!

When you have learnt how to do this, much will be revealed. You'll wonder how you ever got by before you became so well organised. You'll understand why you used to get in such a tangle. Your helpers will come to trust and revere you. Your organisation skills will become legendary. You will arrive calmly at each presentation with nothing left to do but do it. You'll have the game skinned!

Having said that, there are no short cuts and every detail of your presentation preparation will always be your responsibility. No one else's. Yours. There'll be many components which, in time and with good briefings, you can certainly delegate to others—but the ultimate responsibility is yours not theirs.

Nothing so disturbs a presentation as the late arrival of things you should have thought of the day before yesterday. Nothing so ill becomes a presenter as the moment he turns to his hapless helper and hisses, 'Why doesn't this damn gizmo work! I *told* you to check it!!' Indeed, you might have done so but were both your legs broken? Shouldn't *you* have double-checked it, before the presentation? Seems reasonable to me.

What follows assumes that you are the sole presenter because it's easier to explain that way. Later we will deal with double acts and multiple-person presentations. The same basic rules apply to these but there will be additional hints to help you organise these events in harmony.

We've now got a lot to cover—guidelines and check lists and hints on doing this and that and in roughly which order. No matter how thoroughly this is covered, somewhere in the future there will come a presentation which won't quite fit, which will have an element you don't quite know how to handle.

Asking for help

When that moment comes, don't hesitate. Talk to people. Ask around. Never be afraid to do this. After all, not one of us has all the answers to everything, including me, and you.

I used to have an instinct for uncertainty, a peculiar mental mechanism which would trip and I'd get stuck. Sensing when I didn't have enough information to put something together well or in the right order, off I'd go, prowling hither and yon, poking about in books and references, but above all, talking to people, seeking advice.

The moment would always come when the pieces would fall into place, when instinct was satisfied and the job could get going again. Invariably talking to other people gave me the greatest help, because their knowledge and their insights were always different from my own.

So it will be for you, when you are comfortable asking for the help of others. One of the most dangerous misconceptions, especially amongst younger managers, is that to ask a question betrays ignorance. Turn the coin over. Surely questions reveal healthy curiosity, an honest need to know, a real hunger to learn. So, ask away. Show me someone who isn't prepared to help you and I'll show you a real jerk.

By the way, the other real jerks you may run into from time to time—whose attitude should be avoided like the plague—carry the unshakeable conviction that it shouldn't be necessary to ask any questions! These P-plate pinheads have the lofty assumption that they have a right to be *told*, a right to sit back and wait until the free-knowledge ride comes along and to do absolutely nothing to help themselves in the meantime.

It gives me some considerable satisfaction to be able to tell you that such as these invariably miss the bus, are left behind with their grand delusions, overtaken by those of you who go to the trouble to find out. I believe it's called initiative.

15
Setting your objective

Setting the objective for your presentation—deciding precisely what it is you want your presentation to achieve—is the single most important decision you must make before you can construct your presentation to achieve the result you want.

Write your objective down. Write it like a headline, short, sharp and to the point.

Now, review your audience, and assess whether or not your objective is achievable. You must assess whether or not the individuals present will have the authority, the imagination, the financial resources, the need or the greed to respond positively to your proposal.

This parallel review of your objective and your audience will tell you if you have a match, or whether you have some adjustments to

I think they'll go for it, don't you?

make—that is, whether you should modify your objective or, if you are able to do so, to modify the composition of your audience.

If it is entirely your decision who is invited to your presentation, then you have control of the composition of your audience. If, however, key individuals are not available when you need them, or in the reasonably near future, then you have one of three decisions to make:

1. Delay the presentation until they are available.

2. Forget the presentation altogether.

3. Proceed, but with a modified objective.

In considering the third option, a presentation for which the decision-makers are not available, you must decide whether you can usefully influence the remaining members of your audience in favour of your cause. This recognises that they cannot make a decision and it will significantly affect the manner in which you express your objective and construct your presentation. You will now be seeking their support for a course of action, but you will not embarrass them by asking for a decision they do not have the authority to make.

16
Setting the date

The very next items for your preparation check list are the deceptively simple When and Where.

If you have been summoned to make your presentation, then obviously the when and where decisions will have been made for you. All you think you have to do is make sure the instructions are clear and put them in your diary on the right day. Keen students of human frailty, however, will know that there's more to it than that!

For example, if the presentation is to be in your own premises, which happen to have several conference rooms, double check that there hasn't been a change of location between the time you were

TOGA! I thought you said TONGA!

first notified and the great day. Playing last minute hunt-the-audience is going to make you twitchy, hot and late, facing varying degrees of physical and mechanical failure. Not a happy thought!

If your presentation is in other premises, make sure you know exactly where to go and how long it takes to get there. Better to be fifteen minutes early in the car park than fifteen minutes late in a traffic jam and still five kilometres from your destination.

If you are arranging the presentation, then the when and where logistics are your responsibility. However, if certain individuals are crucial to achieving the objective of your presentation, then *their* availability will dictate the date, the time and often the location of your presentation, not the other way round.

Many inexperienced presenters airily set the date and *then* discover that key people are not available. This causes a lot of unnecessary bother before you even get started. Other members of the audience who were available and who accepted your invitation are inclined to get a bit huffy when they learn that the presentation date must be changed so that so-and-so can attend. After all, we all like to think we're important.

'Ah!' you sigh. 'Is nothing simple?' To which the answer is 'Yes, when you think. No, when you don't!'

When it's your deal, 'setting the date' as far in advance as possible has several important advantages to you and to others.

You will control the amount of time you need to prepare and rehearse your presentation.

You will have a reasonable chance of getting the venue you want in which to stage your presentation.

You will have time to book or acquire any equipment you may need and you will be able to give your colleagues and suppliers reasonable advance notice of any products, documents, props or visual aids you'll be likely to need.

The latter point is particularly important. Your thoughtfulness will win you allies every time, so let's look at an example of how this works.

Let's say it's the first of the month today, your presentation is on the twentieth and you think you're going to need roughly a dozen slides. Who's going to get the most co-operation? The panic-merchant who bowls in on the nineteenth, without notice, and howls, 'I must have these by dawn tomorrow!' Or the presenter who calls on the first, advises that slides will be needed, estimates the briefing should be ready by the tenth, delivers on the eleventh, and asks for the slides by the sixteenth—still four days ahead of the presentation, with ample time for revision, if necessary, and for rehearsals.

No contest! You've thought of others, you were well organised early and when the day comes that you do want something in a big hurry, I'd be very surprised if you didn't get full co-operation.

We're making progress! So far we have defined the Objective and reviewed the Audience, set the Date and therefore, established how much Time you have for preparation.

However, there is another missing logistical link to be forged before you can begin to plan your presentation content, and it is also time related. How *long* is your presentation to be and how much time should you allow for the total event, including discussion time at the end of your presentation?

17
The time contract

The length of your presentation depends on whether you have been called upon, or whether you have initiated the presentation.

If you are called upon to make the presentation, then whoever invited you will usually indicate the time available—and if not, ask! You need to know, in order to plan your presentation.

If you are asked to make a brief, ten-minute presentation and you think it should be longer, my advice would be don't argue, just do it. Distill your treasured twenty-minute number down to its key elements and make them as clear and as interesting as you possibly can.

If you've done it well enough, when you've finished you'll get all the questions and discussion you can handle. How much extra time is devoted to this is entirely up to the audience. What you have done is fulfilled your part of the bargain. You complied with your time contract.

A word of caution. Never waste the first few moments making asinine remarks about how hard you're going to try to complete your presentation in the allocated ten minutes. Your audience will have taken that for granted and doing it will earn you more brownie points than saying you're going to try. At all costs resist the temptation of dropping in, 'If I only had more time I could explain this more fully', thereby wasting even more time. It's piteous and in poor taste. Just *do* it and be thankful it's as brief as it is.

On the other hand, if you are allocated what appears to be an excessive amount of time—like two hours when you think one will be more than enough—you may need to question, with some diplomacy, whoever has invited you. Your assumptions on the subject and hers may be very different. Just ask, 'Are there any particular areas you would like to cover?' Then whatever length of presentation you finally settle on, that is your time contract.

If you are the party initiating the presentation, then *you* must estimate the total amount of time you will need and you should always include this information in your invitation.

Keeping in mind that most presentations are too long anyway and that you will confine your presentation to the absolute essentials, a

. . . but I need another half an hour!

useful formula for estimating the total amount of time you will need
is this:

Starting time:	Zero minute
Plus:	Up to but no more than ten minutes for the arrival of stragglers, greetings and introductions, refreshments and opening remarks
Plus:	X minutes for uninterrupted presentation
Plus:	Y minutes for questions and discussion
Plus:	Z minutes for summary of discussion/next action/close/farewells

If X and Y equal fifteen minutes each and Z equals five minutes,
your overall time estimate is approximately forty-five minutes for the
total event, of which only fifteen minutes is occupied by the actual
presentation itself. So, unless you plan to do a real hit-and-run hustle,
do not invite your audience to a 'fifteen minute presentation'. Instead,
indicate that your presentation will occupy about fifteen minutes and

with time allowed for discussion, suggest that your guests allocate about three-quarters of an hour. So, from, say, a nine o'clock start in the morning, they can safely rely on being away by a quarter to ten.

Time estimate/Formula		
Minutes	*Item*	*Example*
0	Starting time	0
0 to 10	Opening	10
plus X	**Presentation**	**15**
plus Y	Questions and discussion	15
plus Z	Summary etc./Close	5
		45 minutes

This is your time contract. It allows both you and your guests to organise the rest of the morning with reasonable confidence. It indicates that you have a proper and business-like regard for the value of time and if your guests decide to stay on and discuss your proposal for longer than you had expected—and that is to your advantage—so be it, as long as you've got your conference room and yourself booked for a little longer than you thought you needed, as a safety margin.

Once you've got your time contract all sorted out, you have enough information to confirm the arrangements made for your presentation.

18
Confirmations

Up to this point it's likely that most of your arrangements will have been made personally or by telephone. While they may have seemed perfectly clear to you, the sorry fact is that we do not all convey or receive information as clearly as we like to think we do. So the time has come to put it in writing, to confirm the details.

A few exceptions

There will be some presentations for which you do not need to do this and as they are few and far between, let's get them out of the way right now.

If you have to make a presentation at very short notice, say in two days time, there's a chance that, under normal circumstances, your presentation will be over before your confirmation has arrived. Personally, I'd do it anyway—and quickly! You can send your memo round by hand, put your letter on a courier or on fax. It takes very little time, signals your efficiency and makes sure everyone's got it straight.

The only other exception is the regular presentation, the weekly, monthly or quarterly gathering, when you are expected to present your results, your plans, or both. For such events location, time, audience composition and the subject of your presentation will be so well known that confirmation would be pedantic and un-necessary.

In all other cases . . .

For all other presentations, whether you have been invited or have initiated, confirmation of the forthcoming event is strongly recommended. Confirmations should always include What (your subject), When, Where, Who and for How Long, plus any additional information which may be relevant. After all, you want your audience as interested and as curious in advance as you can manage.

Let's see how this works. In order to do so, we will have to invent a hypothetical situation and, to demonstrate the differences, we will invite audiences first to an internal and then to an external presentation.

Home and away examples

I would like you to imagine that you are a marketing middle-manager with the Tall Trees Paper Mill, and with your job you have inherited a hideous problem. Due to a mysterious malfunction, the company warehouses are groaning with over-production of high quality, light-weight board, and the other Board is groaning too. Loudly!

Sales of this product have a traditional pre-Christmas peak, but are consistently flat through the rest of the year—and here you are in January, with enough of the blasted stuff to last for ever. Desperate for solutions, the Marketing Director pounces on *you* and commands you to present your ideas and recommendations two weeks from today.

Stung into action, almost immediately you have an idea. In order to make your idea work, you realise that you will need the support and co-operation of Sales, Production and Distribution. Rather than face the prospect of making repetitive presentations, you decide to invite these department heads along too, and get the okay to do so. The confirmation of your verbal arrangement is shown opposite.

As you can see, all the necessary details are concisely covered, and two elements have been added since you were cornered by the Marketing Director.

Firstly, you have taken a positive point of view and expressed the problem as an opportunity in your headline. Then you have clearly stated the objective of your mission in the opening paragraph—that is, not to drag the miserable malfunction through the mud, but to find ways to reduce the inventory. (Exactly *how* you propose to do this will follow in a moment.)

Secondly, you've done some forward thinking, worked out that you're not going to be able to move this paper mountain on your own, and you've wheeled in some helpers. (This could even be considered a bit crafty—witnesses will now be present when you unveil your Great Idea and there'll be no chance of the Marketing Director subsequently taking all the credit!)

What is this great idea? Well, the board in question is the same weight and quality as that supplied to printers for the production of Christmas and birthday greeting cards. In our imaginary example, you have just invented Mother's Day, with all that that implies for the solution to your immediate board problem and for untold opportunities to come.

Needless to say, your idea is received with joy and applause and the discussion turns to the question of not whether you have too much board, but have you enough to meet potential demand!

TALL TREES PAPER MILL INC.

MEMO

Date

From: Marketing Manager/Board

To: Marketing Director

cc: National Sales Manager
Production Manager
Distribution Manager

Re: *Marketing Opportunity For Light Weight Board*

This will confirm that you have asked me to consider and recommend ideas which will result in the significant reduction of our present inventory of Light Weight Board.

This will also confirm that the presentation to you will take place at 4.00 pm on Wednesday, XX Month 19YY in Conference Room No. 1. The presentation is expected to last for approximately one hour, including time for questions and discussion.

Acceptance of one or more of the recommendations which will be made will certainly involve future action by Sales, Production and Distribution. With your approval, therefore, I have also invited the head of each of these departments to join the presentation, and all have agreed to attend.

For reference, copies of all relevant background data, statistics, costs and projections will be provided at the presentation.

(Signature)

Name
Marketing Manager

Note: Titles have been used in this example. Use of names or titles or both will depend on whatever is normal practice in your company.

Not entirely by chance did you time the presentation for 4.00 pm. By 5.30 the champagne corks are flying, and when the fog clears the next morning you are delegated to present this Mother's Day idea to the Biggest & Best Card Corporation. You make contact, arrange the details and send out this confirmation:

TALL TREES PAPER MILL INC.

Date

Mr A. Name,
Marketing Director,
B & B Card Corporation,
ADDRESS

Dear Mr Name,

Greeting Cards: New Product

Following our conversation this morning, this will confirm that we have arranged to make a presentation to you and your colleagues on Monday, XX Month 19YY, at 10.30 am in your office.

As we discussed, TTPM has recently developed an idea which we believe has the potential to lift greeting card sales during what is currently a non-seasonal period, to our mutual advantage.

We estimate that presentation of this idea will take about forty-five minutes, including time for questions and discussion.

Name from TTPM Marketing and Name from TTPM Sales will also be joining me in the presentation, and we look forward very much to seeing you on Monday next. With kind regards,

Yours sincerely,

(Signature)

Name
Marketing Manager

cc: Sales Director, BBCC
New Products Manager, BBCC
Marketing Director, TTPM
National Sales Manager, TTPM

This is brief, polite and to the point. Once again, key details have been covered and enough information supplied to whet the appetite without giving the game away.

These, of course, are not the only ways to write confirmations, and you will develop your own style as time goes by. What is important is that you make clear confirmation a regular practice as part of the preparation you undertake for your presentations. Frankly, neither example is of much use to you—but in both cases the information contained is valuable to others.

19
Organising yourself

Now that you've organised almost everybody else in sight, it's your turn! If you leave your presentation preparation until the last possible moment you'll be in heaps of bother and you and your presentation will be headed for unhappiness.

Busy is no excuse. Everybody's busy! You just have to make time. You have to schedule your preparation time as far in advance as possible, in your own diary, and then you must stick to your arrangements with as much discipline as you can muster.

In your diary you should block off both preparation time and rehearsal sessions—as much time and as many sessions as you think will be necessary.

Later you may have to reschedule some of these, but try to avoid doing this if you can. Otherwise, the presentation date will creep up on you and you'll find yourself dangerously short of preparation time.

Before you can begin the detailed planning of your presentation content, there is one final piece of organisation you have to complete. It's time to go twig gathering.

There's no point in blocking off a couple of hours for your task—firmly closing your ever-open office door behind you, or retreating to your lonely study—if you suddenly realise that without these figures, that flow-chart, or this report you can't do a thing. You should have thought of that before and drop-kicking the cat is not going to make you feel any better!

So, before your content preparation session, make sure you have everything you're likely to need for reference.

You're not going to include all this stuff in your presentation, but you're sure to need various bits of background material against which to check your views of what has gone before, or to help you gaze into the future.

That said, you are now, finally, almost ready to begin preparing the content of your presentation.

Somewhere along the line did you remember to brief your secretary and any assistants you might have? When you have a presentation coming up it's a good idea to share this news, even if you don't think you'll need their help—which I doubt! If nothing else, it will explain your pre-occupation or occasional near catatonic state. If you are going to need twenty bound copies of a document the size of a small novel, your secretary will appreciate knowing about this treasure a little in advance.

20
Organisation check list

Setting your objective and reviewing your audience should always be the first item of organisation. The order in which the other Check List items are completed will vary from one presentation to another.

Item	Action	Completed
Set objective & Review audience	*Either* retain or .... Revise objective	[ ]
Location decisions	Where	[ ]
	When (date)	[ ]
	Starting time	[ ]
Time estimates	Presentation length	[ ]
	Total event length	[ ]
Bookings	Venue	[ ]
	Equipment	[ ]
	Personnel	[ ]
Advance notice	Products	[ ]
	Documents	[ ]
	Props	[ ]
	Visual aids	[ ]
	Other	[ ]
Confirmations	To audience	[ ]
	To colleagues	[ ]
Briefings	Staff	[ ]
	Others with need to know	[ ]
Yourself	Book preparation time/s	[ ]
	Book rehearsal time/s	[ ]
	Gather reference items	[ ]

SECTION

V

Presentation planning

21

Working to format

For some people the very word 'format' may seem too rigid, but I hope to demonstrate how the use of format can save you time and pain and open up creative (and persuasive) possibilities for your future presentations.

Format is really nothing more than the shape of something—the *way* we do things in order to make our task or journey as simple as possible.

For example, books are written' to format, with plot, ideas or information divided into bite-sized pieces. This simplifies both the act of creation and the reader's ability to absorb and enjoy.

Three-act plays are written to format, using the classic pattern of beginning, middle and end. The use of this format frees playwrights' imaginations to concentrate on the *content* of their works, without another moment's concern about the shape they should take. With shape determined, the creative adventure begins.

Thanks to the heroic efforts of our scurvy-ridden ancestors, the maps of our world and the journeys we take today are all dictated by format—with compass points fixed, and longtitude and latitude gridding us across the great continents and oceans. Because it works, when we travel we do not waste our energy reinventing navigation. We simply sit back and enjoy the ride.

So, too, can format help you with the planning of your future presentations. Every presentation will, of course, differ in its subject and content but for each the milestones of the journey can be the same.

Working to format when you are preparing your future presentations will give you these advantages:

- You will save time and anxiety by not having to fret about the shape.

- You will know where and how to begin. No more glaring into the middle distance, or gazing dolefully at blank sheets of paper.
- With format clear, your energy and creativity can be poured into the persuasive content of your presentation.
- Your thinking will be more clearly focussed on how best you can achieve your presentation objective.
- You will be better able to plan how your presentation is to end—which is at least as important as how it got started!

Now, with the fear of 'how' replaced by the excitement of 'what', you will have the opportunity to approach your presentation in a much more relaxed and positive frame of mind. The end result of that relaxation and enthusiasm will become evident in the skill, good humour and sincerity with which you will ultimately present your case.

Thinking in headlines

For planning a presentation to format, we are not concerned with fine detail, only with outline—and at this stage of planning great self-control is called for, to avoid drifting off into patches of purple prose.

We are first going to think only in headlines. Let me explain.

Visualise, if you will, the front page of your daily newspaper made up *only* of text. No headlines. Only column after column of grey words on grey paper, all in the same small type. Where do you start? How do you find the stories that interest or affect you without searching up and down each column, prowling every centimetre of the page? This would really test the eye!

Now visualise your front page as you actually confront it every day and see the difference. Bold headlines signal every story. You can see what's up in a single glance.

This, then, is how we're going to shape your presentations, by planning the content in *headlines.* Once you are satisfied with the clarity and correctness of your headlines, with the relevance and logic of your format, then the rest is going to be dead easy.

Opposite is a simple, practical format for planning any presentation, with the added advantage of flexibility. Somewhat in the fashion of the click-together building blocks for children, it can have bits removed or extended, as circumstances dictate. Let us look first at the overall shape and then review each component in turn.

Presentation planning format

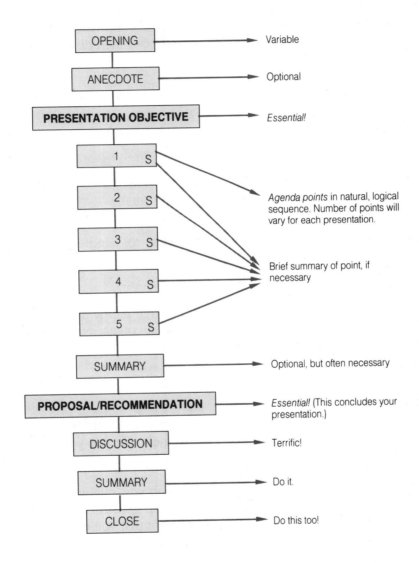

OPENING	Variable
ANECDOTE	Optional
PRESENTATION OBJECTIVE	*Essential!*
1 S	
2 S	*Agenda points* in natural, logical sequence. Number of points will vary for each presentation.
3 S	
4 S	Brief summary of point, if necessary
5 S	
SUMMARY	Optional, but often necessary
PROPOSAL/RECOMMENDATION	*Essential!* (This concludes your presentation.)
DISCUSSION	Terrific!
SUMMARY	Do it.
CLOSE	Do this too!

Opening

The Opening is the settling-down phase of your presentation. It provides an opportunity for you to gather attention and to state any ground rules you may wish to make clear. It allows you to strike a balance between waffling to the start of your presentation, or starting too abruptly. It is also a moment for you to extend courtesy to your audience. It is where you should identify your subject (as distinct from your Objective), to remind your audience why they're there.

So, depending on the circumstances and each individual audience, your Opening headline notes (for yourself) can include all or some of the following:

- Courtesies — Greetings/thanks to audience for attending
- Acknowledgements — Everyone is present/you are ready to begin
- Logistics — Time contract
  Refreshment details
  Organisational details
- Subject — Of presentation
- Questions — How you want to handle them (see Chapter 22)

When you become an experienced presenter, handling the Opening phase will be second nature. On the way to that happy day, however, it is strongly recommended that you plan what you are going to cover carefully and include your opening remarks in your notes and rehearsals.

Anecdote

It's often a useful idea to create a bridge between your Opening and your Objective and humour can be an extremely effective way of doing this—if you can handle it, if the humour is relevant to your subject and if it is appropriate to your audience.

Most of us enjoy a good chuckle, although you might think twice about getting jolly with a group of gulag camp guards or a gathering of income tax inspectors—in the unlikely event that you were to make a presentation to either! Let common sense prevail and, above all, assess your audience beforehand.

Use of anecdote as a connecting link between your subject and your Objective is not obligatory. It can certainly ease tension and focus attention when done well and if you decide to take this route then the headline for your planning notes need be nothing more than a key phrase or the punchline of your anecdote.

Presentation objective

This is it, folks! This is the statement of what you want to achieve in your presentation. Write it down. Polish it until you are certain it says what you mean and you mean what you say, and then do not deviate from it. Above all, keep it short, and keep it simple. Write it as a headline.

This is the moment for absolute clarity—for yourself, and later for your audience. This is the very foundation of your presentation. It is the proposal to which you are seeking agreement, action and reaction.

It is likely that you will use a visual aid for your Objective, to focus the attention of your audience. So when you have perfected your Objective, look at it again with the visual aspect in mind. Sketch it out. Stand back and look at it (as best you can) through the eyes of your audience. Does it still mean what you thought it did? Does it have both intellectual *and* visual impact?

This, your Objective, is your banner headline. It is always the very first thing you should prepare in planning your presentation so it is well worth the trouble you will take to get it absolutely right.

Agenda points

The items you choose for your Agenda are the building blocks which will connect your Objective to your Proposal/Recommendation.

How many items you will need will depend entirely on the type of presentation you are making, the complexity of your argument and on the extent of the existing knowledge of your audience.

The expected attitude of your audience may also play a part in your choice of agenda points. An audience which you believe may be reluctant to accept your proposal is likely to take somewhat more persuading than one with a positive predisposition to your idea and this may affect the construction of your agenda.

Start drafting. Write down the 'headlines' of your agenda points in the sequence that feels right to you. Then, with your Objective in front of you, double-check the agenda and, if necessary, revise it until you are confident that you have covered each point that is important to your argument. Then check to be sure that you've got them in the right order, to help your audience follow the logical path of your reasoning. (How long you will spend on each point is not relevant here, although it's likely you will have a good idea which items will be brief and which will be lengthy.)

Now you have your agenda headlines, and you're looking good!

Summary

On our Presentation Planning Format chart this item is described as 'optional'. However, in my experience it is usually both necessary and desirable to draw the threads of your argument together before you come to your final recommendation for action.

After all, you may have explored, say, five or more different aspects of your problem or opportunity, and these must have been inter-related or you wouldn't have included them in the first place! You know that, and you will have covered each point clearly, but it's always possible that one or some of your audience might have missed the connection. So a brief Summary is often a good move, just to make sure everyone's got the message—and as a springboard into your Proposal/Recommendation.

At this early planning stage, the outline of your presentation need only include the headline word Summary, if you are going to include one. You can write the actual statement later, when you are preparing your material in detail.

Indeed you should do so. This is no point at which to waffle! Your Summary will need to be as crystal clear as will your Objective and Proposal/Recommendation.

Proposal/Recommendation

This is your destination. This is the big finish—the recommendation you will leave ringing in the ears of your audience at the end of your presentation, and it needs to be as unequivocal as the statement of the Objective with which you began.

Often the words you use in your Proposal/Recommendation will be almost identical to those you used for your Objective. At other times they may be somewhat modified, as you can now draw on the evidence you have presented throughout your agenda.

Write down your Proposal/Recommendation statement as concisely as you possibly can—headline style! Sometimes you can do this at the same time as you prepare your Objective, at other times as soon as you have roughed out your Agenda. Whenever you do it, do it you must. This is where you are heading throughout your presentation. This is where you 'ask for the order'.

'What!!', I hear you cry. 'I'm not *selling* anything!'

Yes you are, and don't you forget it! The fact that so many shy away from the idea of 'selling' is the very reason why so many presentations collapse in a soggy heap at the end, leaving untold numbers of audiences wondering vaguely what to do next.

If you believe in the topic of your presentation, in your idea, in your vision of doing something differently, and you want others to agree, then you have to *persuade* them and you have a right to propose what should happen next.

'Ask for the order' may be a somewhat blunt expression, but it leaves us in no doubt that you have thought through your presentation very carefully, and this is what you want to happen.

By making this clear to your audience you are helping them to understand and decide and helping your presentation to succeed.

Having 'asked for the order' your presentation is over—and the fun's about to begin!

Discussion

Now, your audience has been bottling up its reactions right through your presentation and it's time for them to cut loose and make their contribution—but it's much too soon for you to sink back into a state of happy exhaustion and relief. You've still got lots to do!

It's time to remain alert and to listen, listen, listen. There may be questions directed to you, many of which you will wish to answer, and both the questions and the answers will provoke more discussion between the members of the audience.

In that sense you now become one of the group rather than the sole performer. If you learn to listen carefully to the post-presentation exchanges, you will often discover great richness of views and useful information, some of which may be quite new to you.

You will also be able to observe who amongst your audience is responding favourably to your proposal and who is uncertain, and at this point you may be able to add a persuader or two.

It is not at all uncommon for members of your audience to start persuading each other, answering each other's questions without waiting for you to do it. This is a healthy sign that you've really got them going. Don't try to grab centre stage again. Sit back and let 'em do it!

Summary

Keep listening, making notes as appropriate, because when the moment is right, it is both necessary and businesslike to summarise the discussion which has just taken place, before your audience slips out of your grasp. If follow-up tasks are allocated, next get-togethers proposed, dates indicated, it's up to you to tie up the loose ends and confirm that everyone understands.

This is your post-discussion Summary and if your presentation has provoked interested and excited discussion and it's clear that Things Are Going to Happen, then your Summary of the discussion can be the high point of your week!

Close

Now there is just one final step for you to take—one which is often overlooked by presenters. Just as you opened your presentation on a courteous note, so you should plan to conclude your presentation in the same way—usually immediately on the heels of your Summary of the Discussion.

It's time to thank your audience sincerely for their time, attention and contributions, and to indicate that the meeting has now finished. (The way you choose your words will depend, of course, on the outcome of your presentation.)

Even if you lost, stiffen the sinews and politely close the meeting. No one likes a sore loser, and skulking off with your files and thumping the door behind you is only likely to reinforce the audience's impression that they were right in the first place!

After all, no matter what the outcome, your audience did attend, they did listen and they did decide. They have a right to expect your appreciation of that.

22
Questions to be considered

Before we go any further, let us have a look at the question of questions, an element of making presentations which can be troublesome to many presenters.

The worries about questions seem to exist at many levels—a sort of mish-mash of fear and confusion. There is the fear of being interrupted by questions, even the fear of not being asked any questions at all, and the fear of not being able to handle them when they do arrive. So let's get these fears out in the open and out of the way.

You are the expert

Always remember, you are the expert. Not the only one by any means, but by the time you have put all your thought and energy into your presentation, you are going to be very well-informed indeed on your subject.

You will probably be better informed than most members of your audience, for the simple reason that you have been burrowing about in your topic much more deeply and much more recently than others, and with greater purpose than anyone else who will be present.

This can be a most comforting revelation! No matter that members of your audience may sometimes have grander titles and greyer hair— on your topic, for your presentation, *you are the expert*. So, what do you really have to fear? Your expertise is in great shape, and you will do well to remember that.

You have every reason to have confidence in your own ability to answer any fair question that comes your way. There is no reason to panic if a question arises. Chances are better than good that you'll have the answer.

Let's now look at the fear of interruption.

It's your call

This is *your* presentation and in your Opening you have the opportunity to set the ground rules, and you have a perfect right to ask for the co-operation of your audience.

Let's say that you have a twenty-minute presentation to make, covering a series of inter-connected agenda points, and it's important for you to complete your presentation in one hit. Politely but firmly in your Opening remarks you can ask for questions to be held until the end of your presentation. You can say, for example:

> *I'm sure you will have questions about some of the ideas and material*
> *I am going to be presenting to you today. Some of these may be answered*
> *by the presentation itself, as we go along . . . and I would appreciate*
> *it if you could hold your questions until the end. We can then have*
> *a thorough discussion at that point. Thank you.*

Most audiences will respect your wishes. After all, you've signalled your preference and prepared the way for *their* presentation behaviour. This tells them to get out their pads and note any questions arising. This is a short presentation and your request for tolerance is quite reasonable.

Let's now imagine that there's a maverick in the mob, who either forgets your request or gets so excited that he or she just has to interrupt with a question. How do you handle that?

Firstly, remember that it's your presentation. It's *your* choice how you respond, and you *do* have options.

- You can answer immediately and fully, but this may very well put you in danger of interrupting the flow of your presentation and opening the door to others. This is definitely not recommended.

- If truthfully the question relates to a point coming up, then say so. Acknowledge the question, and simply state that the answer will emerge shortly.

- Now, if it happens to be a point you'd never even considered, above all, *do not panic*! Pause, perhaps scribble a note to yourself, and acknowledge. 'That's a most interesting question', you say. 'Thank you. I'd like to come back to that after the presentation, if I may.' Or words to that effect.

Keep rolling. Do not let yourself get side-tracked into discussion during short presentations.

For presentations extending over much longer periods, you must plan to deal with questions in a different manner. It is unreasonable to expect that you can lock-up an audience for an hour or longer and muzzle them throughout, nor is it desirable to do so. Either frustration will build and threaten to erupt or those in the quieter corners of the room will be catching the odd forty winks.

Controlling questions in longer presentations is partly a matter of agenda construction and partly a matter of your direction to the audience.

Agenda items for longer presentations will obviously be more lengthy than for the shorter versions and you may need to make a Summary at the end of each point. This is where questions can be invited on the point just covered. Having dealt with questions on that issue and got your audience nicely involved in that aspect, you can then move cheerfully along to the next.

This kind of audience management will allow you to keep control of your presentation through the planned placement of question times, and not allow it to degenerate into uncontrolled discussion and run-away wisdom.

Pausing

I have seen presenters respond to questions like mackerels in a feeding frenzy! They get so excited, so on top of their subject, that when a query comes their way they snap off the answer before the dot has landed under the question mark.

While the answer may be quite correct, this manner of reply is downright awful. It makes the answer seem slick and ill-considered, and often appears insulting to the questioner, who has every right to expect that his or her tender question is deserving of some consideration.

Pause, my friends. Pause before you answer. Let the thought of the question have its moment in the sun. It may be that your pause may allow another (either a colleague or a member of the audience) to answer the question, perhaps even better than you can do.

If *you* answer the question, then your pause will allow you a moment to mentally scan your reply options and choose before you answer.

If you don't know

If you really don't know the answer to a question, say so. There's no loss of face in doing so, especially if it's a really good question in an area you'd never even considered.

A sincere acknowledgement of a good question is a far better response than trying to fake a fudgy answer. Own up, and cover the moment (after your pause), with a response such as:

> *That's a really interesting question. I honestly don't know the answer to that—let me think about it (or look into it) and I'll get back to you.*

You're being honest. The asker will be pleased, and you have a perfect opportunity for follow-up contact.

If you don't know what a question *means*, ask for it to be put again. It's quite fair to do so, and may very well help the questioner too. He or she may not have got it quite right the first time and others may well be equally puzzled. You then serve as the means by which the question is clarified.

If you get lost

I can remember once getting a weird and rather tangled question (which I should have clarified and didn't) in a post-presentation discussion. I thought I understood it, more or less, and thought I had at least half an answer. Wrong on both counts!

Off I wandered, meandering about, getting in a bigger mess by the minute and seeing the furrows deepen in the brows of the struggling audience.

'Oh, my God!' I moaned, suddenly. 'I've forgotten the question!' So I had—and so had everyone else—and in the laughter that followed we moved along to the next.

Forgiveness and understanding is, thankfully, alive and well when we do make a mess of it. There's nothing that's going to happen to you in a presentation that hasn't happened to everyone else in the room at some time—and in the many years that I have made presentations I cannot remember a single occasion when a question was ever asked with real malice.

Curly questions

Amongst less experienced folk the most commonly asked question is, 'How do you deal with curly (or tricky) questions?'

Well, I don't believe that there *are* any curly or tricky questions, because implicit in those words is the belief that the asker is somehow out to trip you up, to make your life a misery and to condemn your bright career to a lifetime of filing duties. Rubbish!

There will be hard questions. There will be bright questions, tough questions, stupid questions and badly-put questions—even questions to which the answer (to you) is so blindingly obvious you may be dumbfounded it was even asked.

To all of these, quite simply you will either be able to provide an answer or you will not. If you do not know the answer there are sensible ways of dealing with this, as we have seen and believe me, the world is not going to come to a grinding halt if you cannot respond on the spot.

You must always remember that the audience for your presentation is not your adversary, and by virtue of your preparation *you* are the expert on your topic. You can take comfort and courage from this certain knowledge.

The final insurance you can take out against the prospect of unexpected questions is to play the devil's advocate with your own material, as you are preparing it and during your rehearsals.

Preparation is your best defence

When you've got your presentation well under way, take a good look at it from the point of view of the individuals who will be in your audience. Ask yourself which aspects are of special interest to which people; what are they likely to want to know that you may not have fully covered.

This doesn't mean that you start stuffing all that information back into your presentation, only that you prepare yourself for questions on this or that point, if they come up. By quizzing your own material, if you do find a soft spot, a missing link, then you have ample time to fix it before the great day.

Your answers will be as well-informed as they can possibly be.

No questions?

What if there is deathly silence, no questions? How do you deal with this? Is it okay?

Often it *is* okay. It's important to keep an open mind on the subject, and to try to avoid feeling fraught if questions do not arise.

Sometimes a presentation will have been so clear and concise that questions will be unnecessary and a decision will be given right away. Sometimes, rather than respond immediately to such a clear proposal, the audience may prefer to think about it overnight and respond later. This is okay.

Sometimes your audience will be weighing your Proposal/ Recommendation, still absorbing it after you have finished speaking. If this is obviously the case then give them a moment to gather their thoughts and shuffle their papers before probing for questions. This is also okay. In fact, it's a very good sign if the audience is clearly digesting what you have said.

Some audiences really do find it difficult to get started with questions and the reasons for this differ widely. Sometimes no one wants to go first! Or more junior individuals wait for the top brass to begin— and sometimes vice versa. Sometimes people are just as tentative about asking questions as presenters are nervous about receiving them!

If you sense that an audience is having difficulty getting started, and you *do* want a discussion of your idea to follow your agenda point or complete presentation, then in this case it will be up to you to draw the questions out.

To do this you will have to use leading questions in order to get your audience talking—those questions which cannot be answered with a simple yes-no answer but which require a reaction. You know them. The ones that go:

How do you feel about . . . ?

What would happen if . . . ?

When do you think we could . . . ?

What would it take to . . . ?

Shy or conservative audiences may take a moment or two to get going but they will respond to leading questions, because they must. The next thing you know they'll be talking to you and talking amongst themselves and your next problem may be getting them to stop! That, of course, you will do with your Summary, when the excitement starts to abate.

Questions are good news

Questions about your presentations are good news and should not be feared as mean and spiteful arrows. They are the flags of interest, the signals of involvement, often gifts of insight and understanding.

So if you can adopt the attitude of openness, if you have prepared for questions as thoroughly as you possibly can, then question-and-discussion time in your presentations can be as interesting and enjoyable as any everyday conversation you have with friends and close associates.

Questions mean that out there in your audience people were listening and they cared enough to ask for more. That's definitely good news.

Now that we've discussed working to format and dealing with questions in some detail, let's have a look at a couple of examples of how all this fits together.

23
Format examples

Let's now look at two examples of outlines for presentations—one short and one much longer. For each of these we will once again explore imaginary situations.

A short presentation

For our short presentation example we're going to explore an idea for cleaning up domestic dogs, and I would like you to imagine that you are a bright young engineer working for a huge multinational which has carved its niche in the world cleaning up everything else in sight, including the opposition.

Your company produces terrific products which clean clothes and kitchens, babies and bathrooms, hair and skin and, over the years, to this impressive array of cleansers has been added a further range of successful softeners, conditioners and deodorisers—in powders and liquids, and bottles and sprays of limitless variety.

The human population and its habitat is now about as purified as it's going to get, but the relentless search for company growth goes on, ever demanding new product ideas. Months have passed and notions have been hard to come by. In our perfect world in which the good idea doesn't care who had it, you've got one—and the fact that you're supposed to work with a slide rule not a television script is neither here nor there.

Your boss (who is the Technical Director and a thoroughly good chap) thinks you're on to something and arranges for you to make a short presentation of your idea to the weekly meeting of the working directors, a gathering which includes the folk responsible for Marketing, Sales, R&D and Finance.

Fifteen minutes is not very long to present a big idea to a busy group, so you'll have no time to go wool-gathering. Your Objective, your Agenda and your Proposal/Recommendation will have to be clear. So let's see firstly what you believe and then we'll construct your presentation outline.

The 'Deodorisation of dogs'

You don't particularly like dogs but you do have a particular interest in social progress, in the way people live, in the effects of urban stress and in potential solutions.

You are aware of the growth of the aged segment of the population and of the decline of the extended family—resulting in increasing numbers of older people living in smaller accommodation, in greater social isolation and loneliness than ever before. Their plight touches you.

As well as this, you've registered the growing body of evidence which suggests that dog ownership is both emotionally and physically beneficial to the elderly and is being more and more frequently recommended by doctors and social workers.

So, here's your big idea. The domestic dog population is on the rise and for good reason! Beloved and desirable these woofers may be but they get very smelly at both ends and pollute the sparkling domestic habitat your company has spent years and trillions cleaning up. Logically there seems no reason why your company's product expertise and technology cannot now turn its attention to Old Spot—and by chance you know just the vets to help you do it.

So, that's the background to your idea. Let's see how this translates into your presentation format, starting with your Objective on the one hand and your Audience Review on the other. After some thought you decide that you want the directors to:

Consider

Deodorants for Dogs

for priority inclusion in the

New Products Development Programme

That's okay, but not quite good enough. So, after some further thought you decide to change it to a more positive Objective. You don't want them to *consider* it, you want them to *do* it! You want them to:

> Include
>
> ***Deodorants for Dogs***
>
> in the New Products
> Development Programme

Happy, now, with your Objective, you turn to your Audience Review, to check that your Objective is achievable, and to review who does what and what does each need to know. Briefly, you conclude:

Objective: Achievable—decision-makers will be present. Although senior, all known to be receptive. Anxious for new product opportunities and will be interested. Will be primed in advance by Technical Director, who will support. Key decision-makers, Marketing & R&D.
Note:
1. New product ideas a problem world-wide. If new idea successful here, all will receive head office/international recognition!
2. All have dogs in own family environment.

Marketing: Sharp and precise—likes ideas supported by numbers. Responsible for acceptance of idea, initiating/managing project, and for funding from development budget.
Note: Provide trend statistics for aged population and dog registrations' growth, plus copies all support data/articles re benefits of pet ownership.

R&D: Closer to Technical than others—likely to be surprised/ pleased by idea from Engineering! Anxious for new project—staff under-utilised. May fret about lack of veterinary personnel in company.

               Note: Supply credentials of veterinary consultants and refer to veterinary options (R&D selection).

Technical: On side and pleased—one-up on Marketing! Attitude: you-invent-it-we'll-make-it. Will support and will acknowledge this in presentation.

Sales: Development timing too long-range for immediate concern. Will be weighing extra burden of work-load on sales team versus opportunity for big launch/trade impact and goodwill. Too early for opinion to have real weight—but opposition could be awkward.

Finance: Sole interest, financial projections.

               Note: Include first phase development cost estimate, even rough.

Your Audience Review now completed, you conclude that your revised Objective is still achievable—and you have gained some valuable guidelines for the likely shape of your Agenda and for the documents and data you will need to support your proposal. You decide that, in order to achieve your Objective, your Proposal/ Recommendation will be an action statement. So, you put it all together, and on page 94 we see how your complete outline emerges, in headline form.

Hereafter three things are going to happen.

Firstly, working to your outline, you've got to get all the solid preparation of your presentation sorted out—data, statistics, documents, visual aids and props. (See chapter dealing with Step-by-Step Preparation.) Of course you will rehearse until you are word perfect!

Secondly, you will make your presentation.

Thirdly, having done so, and having savoured the stunned and appreciative silence that follows your Proposal/Recommendation— the split second before all hell breaks loose—you will then join in the animated and approving discussion which follows. (Perhaps you may begin to wonder if your casual social observations and your disapproval of the offending orifices of man's best friends may not have changed your career path for ever.)

OPENING

Thanks: For chance to present idea.

Time: About 15 minutes/5 minutes for questions.

Questions: Please hold to end.

Subject: New product opportunity in the pet care market—a unique product idea to make household dogs more socially acceptable using our existing deodorant expertise and technology.

ANECDOTE

Woof and Poof story*

OBJECTIVE

(Persuade you to . . .) include **Deodorants for Dogs**

in the New Products Development Programme

AGENDA

1. **Social Trends:** Aging population/reduced living space/social isolation/loneliness
2. **Therapeutic Benefits of Dog Ownership:** Physical—exercise and social contact
                                           Psychological—companionship
3. **Domestic Problem:** Dog odours (oral and anal)
4. **Product Opportunity:** Oral and anal deodorants
5. **Market Target Groups:** Retirees/elderly (primary). Families (secondary)
6. **Technical:** Existing expertise and technology
7. **Product Development:** Veterinary consultants (credentials and options)
8. **Action Plan:** (a) Veterinary consultations/product feasibility
                      (b) Estimates of potential market size
                      (c) Product concept/consumer attitude research
                      (d) Timing estimate to assessment stage/six weeks
9. **Cost Estimate:** Preliminary

SUMMARY

Evidence suggests that an opportunity exists to develop a new cosmetic segment of the pet care market, with entry via Dog Deodorants. If our Dog Deodorant products are vet-feasible, we can banish woof and poof problems for ever—and certainly profit by it! Therefore, I propose:

PROPOSAL/RECOMMENDATION

That Dog Deodorants be included in the new products development programme and that you adopt the action plan proposed today.

---

* This rather puts me in mind of a news item I saw the other day, reporting an incident at the famous Crufts Dog Show. It was the turn of the Old English Sheepdogs to be shown and out they came, with their full coats all tizzed and blow-dried, looking like black-and-white fuzz balls on parade.

     One of the older judges, renowned for his short-sightedness, startled a proud owner by trying to check his entrant's eyes from the wrong end! Challenged, he replied, 'My sincere apologies, old man, but with these chaps it's frightfully difficult to tell which end woofs and which end poofs!'

     (Introduction to Objective then follows: 'Now, ladies and gentlemen, I believe that we have a new product opportunity for both the end that woofs and the end that poofs, and today I want to persuade you to . . .')

Finally, of course, it will be up to you to Summarise any decisions taken in the Discussion and then Close, with thanks.

If I were making this presentation—knowing that every member of my audience was a dog owner—I would then pass out a gift-wrapped souvenir to each (one of those rolled-hide imitation dog bones sold in pet shops, I think), for each to take home as an offering. Of such gestures memories are made.

A long presentation

With another imaginary example we're now going to look at a long presentation, in order to discover the ways in which this differs from a short one.

As we shall see, other than the overall length, the main differences between the two relate to the needs of the audience—and because you too are only human, to your own needs in an extended period of concentration.

Over time, maintaining concentration is difficult for us all, so for these longer presentations we must find special ways to encourage and hold audience attention.

For longer presentations it is also very important to consider the comfort of your audience, to consider their physical needs for refreshment and breaks. When these are well organised and correctly positioned in the agenda, they can add considerably to the well-being of everybody!

This must all be preplanned and managed in such a way that there is no significant interference with the flow of your presentation and therefore agenda construction and time management play a much more important role than for a short presentation, which can easily be conducted without either interruption or fatigue.

As for a short presentation, your first task is still the definition of your Objective combined with your Audience Review. When these are clear, you then draft your Agenda and your Proposal/Recommendation.

Having done so, and having estimated the amount of time you will need to cover each item, you must then very carefully review your Agenda again. With this review you will now:

- Estimate and add a time allowance for questions and discussion at the conclusion of individual agenda points, where it is appropriate. (Some points will be so factual you will conclude that questions are either unlikely or are uncalled for. For other points, which may cover new or contentious areas, you can bet the bankroll that questions will pop up all over. On others you may wish to draw out questions in order to involve members of the audience in that aspect of your presentation.) Then:

- With your Agenda retimed point by point to include questions and discussion, you can determine the approximate overall length of your presentation. You must decide whether or not you need or wish to include a break, and if you do, where it is going to be the least disruptive.

Carefully estimated Agenda timing will also help you to check on your overall timing while there is still time to change it, and it may indicate that either an earlier or later start to your presentation is necessary.

Timing traps and troubles

For example, if your presentation was initially planned for high noon in the boardroom, and the draft of your timed Agenda clearly shows that you're going to need an hour and three-quarters, you have a problem looming. By the time you've hit your big finish it will be a quarter to two, and your audience will be faint with hunger. If you want the undivided attention of that audience, you'd better start thinking about starting earlier or postponing until after lunch.

For a presentation of that length it's unlikely that you would welcome the noisy, bothersome interruption of a catered lunch for the group. Relatively silent sandwiches are less disruptive. However, while your audience will be able to munch-and-listen, *you* will not, and when the time arrives for discussion at the end of your presentation proper, you may be facing a serious energy crisis. In these circumstances rescheduling your start time is strongly recommended.

For an even longer presentation of, say three to four hours, if you want to avoid a major refreshment break, such as a lunch, clearly you will need to start either early in the morning or early in the afternoon. You will still need to plan for the inclusion of a break, or risk having audience members wandering in and out at will. However, with your timed Agenda you can dictate exactly *when* this is to occur and, of course, advise your audience of this happy fact in your Opening remarks.

With those thoughts in mind, let's have a look at who you are and what you're up to this time, with this imaginary Long Presentation.

The 'Great lettuce seed crisis'

Let us imagine that you are an experienced agronomist, one of several employed by a large Australian producer and distributor of seeds. Your company markets packet seeds for household gardens. However, by far the greater part of their business is in the development, sale and distribution of hardy, reliable seeds for commercial crops of flowers and vegetables. Your company raises and harvests these seeds on their own land, throughout the country.

Your particular speciality is in green leaf crops. You are the Lettuce Whiz, the acknowledged expert in all the many varieties grown in climatic areas which range from the steamy north to the chilly south, from areas of abundant water to the semi-arid fringes of the outback.

All is well in your southern land, but in the Northern Hemisphere wild and eccentric weather begins the destruction of the spring lettuce crop. By blazing mid-summer the destruction is complete. Salad is off the northern menu, and all lettuce seed-crops for the next season's planting have failed. The effect on northern nutrition and on the future prospects of growers is bordering on catastrophic.

Your main sowing and seed-raising season in the Southern Hemisphere is approaching. The practice of distributing crop-seeds internationally, by air, is well established. And a shoe box full of tiny seeds is a lot of lettuce, whichever way you look at it!

So, fully aware of the problem to the north, and with motives ranging from avarice to altruism, the folks in your company call you on your field phone and ask you, the lettuce expert, to 'make a presentation'. They set aside half a day to hear your review, two weeks from today.

Recognising a wide-open and woolly brief when you hear one, you know right away that in order to focus your presentation you need more information.

So, somewhat peeved—and with every right to be so—you hop into your four-wheel drive, hasten to head office, bail up the briefer, and after some rather intense discussion you discover that what everyone really wants to know, in the light of the northern problem, is:

1. What can the company do?
2. To what extent can they do it
   (a) on current plan and
   (b) with extra effort/new plan?
3. What's the bottom line?

They don't want you to waffle about winds and weather and what-if. It's now clear that your presentation is going to be about inventory, varietal yield forecasts, alternative action plans, human and financial resources and, above all, about taking decisions.

You conclude that reaching decisions on action can be the only realistic, achievable Objective for your presentation and decide to announce this to your audience with this proposal, asking them to:

**Agree to
supply the needs of the
Northern Hemisphere
for the coming season**

Your plan is to include all the details of how, to what extent and at what estimated cost, in the body of your presentation, so that your audience will then be in a position to respond favourably (or not)—and immediately. The germinating lettuce seed is not going to sit around waiting for anyone!

We must pause here, of course, to review the audience members, and this time *you* can fill in all the individual characteristics of attitudes and expected response you think would apply to the folks in this company, in this industry and on this topic. It's good practice for you! Your audience will consist of the Managing Director, the Chief Agronomist, and department heads responsible for agricultural sales, import/export and finance, with each of the latter three accompanied by a helper.

You are now free to test your audience conclusions against the Objective, and if you want to change it, go right ahead. Since my purpose, however, is to demonstrate the planning, construction and time-management of a long presentation, I'm going to stick with what I have, draft my Agenda and determine detailed and overall timing.

The natural immediate thought for first agenda point is background, a review of the problem. Now, that could take *hours*, and in this case can be trimmed right back. To bring knowledge up to the same level for all participants, we'll promptly decide to circulate existing and expert reports in advance. This will avoid boring the knowledgeable, help the needy, and save heaps of time in the presentation itself.

That fixed it's back to the Planning Format and drafting the Agenda, and the outline and timing estimates look like this:

Lettuce presentation	Approximate presentation time (minutes) 1st estimate	Approximate presentation time Revised estimate
Opening and Objective	10	10
Agenda		
1. Northern Hemisphere/Overview	~~20~~	10
2. Company inventory x varieties	~~15~~	10
3. Varieties x NH suitability	~~30~~	15
4. International distribution	~~20~~	15
5. Export plan/Current surplus	10	10
6. Export plans (3)/Increased yields	~~45~~	30
7. Unresolved issues	~~25~~	20
8. Export plans, personnel/logistics	~~15~~	10
Presentation **Summary**	10	10
Recommendation	5	5
	3.25 hours	2.25 hours
Discussion	±30	±30
Summary and Close	5	5
Total estimated time:	4.00 hours	3.00 hours

(handwritten notes: "2 hours + SQD"; "Too long!"; "4.00" circled)

The first estimated timing of the Agenda spotlights a problem. The presentation is too long. You still have to add back time for SQD

(Summary, Questions and Discussion) at the end of all or some of the individual Agenda points, and also plan for a mid-presentation break.

Now it's time to balance obligation and discipline—the obligation to be clear against the discipline of being brief—and of showing mercy to the audience in the process!

As you hack back your timing from four hours to three, you realise that you want to make this presentation in the afternoon, not the morning. A two o'clock start is what you need. You *must* estimate your timing, but you're not running a railroad—and if really useful discussion of good ideas is taking place, the last thing you want to do is chop that off prematurely. So, for a long presentation, an afternoon start provides a better opportunity to run into reasonable overtime than the morning option.

So, back to the timing plan, and let's see what happens when a break is added and when SQDs are put in place in your Agenda:

Lettuce presentation	Approximate presentation time	
	Revised estimate	SQD plus break
Agenda	Minutes	Minutes
1. Northern Hemisphere/Overview	10	—
2. Company inventory x varieties	10	5
3. Varieties x NH suitability	15	5
4. International distribution	15	5
Break	—	15
5. Export plan/Current surplus	10	—
6. Export plans (3)/Increased yields	30	10
7. Unresolved issues	20	10
8. Export plans, personnel/logistics	10	5
Agenda presentation time	2 hours	
SQD and Break time		55 minutes
Total Agenda time:	2 hours and	55 minutes*

* Plus your previously estimated 1 hour of time for Opening, Objective and the items following your Agenda, a total of 3 hours and 55 minutes for the full presentation. A long one indeed!

For this presentation you have positioned your break for refreshments about one hour and fifteen minutes in, and placed it between the last Agenda point dealing with the present, and the first which will reach into the future—the only natural place for it to occur without risking disruption of the flow. You are conscious that some of your SQD timing may be a bit brief, but you have allowed for overall overtime by deciding to hold the presentation in the afternoon.

Now, other than the step-by-step preparation of your presentation, your overall planning is almost complete. All that remains is to put together your complete Agenda, with all the timing details and sub-heads in there. When that is done, you will have both a detailed map to follow, and the means of clearly briefing those whose help you will need in searching and checking, in helping to get to the start.

When planning a long presentation, I strongly favour an easy-to-follow, working master plan, with a page for each section, a good, open layout and lots of room for scribbling! A few minutes spent preparing this can be time well spent. For the Great Lettuce Presentation, this is what it should include:

Page 1:   Cover
Page 2:   Presentation outline & timing
Page 3:   Opening
Page 4:   Anecdote & Objective
Page 5/6:   Agenda
Page 7:   Summary & Recommendation

The following pages show how it would look.

Cover (which also reminds you to confirm the presentation, book the conference room, warn the tea server, *and* gives you a ready-made list to check off your audience as they arrive):

Northern Hemisphere Lettuce
Produce & Seed-Crop Failure

Presentation to: Managing Director

Chief Agronomist

Manager, Agricultural Sales

Manager, Import/Export

Financial Director

Agricultural Sales Assistant

Import/Export Assistant

Commercial Assistant

Date:.......................................

Time: 2.00 pm

Place: Head Office, Conference Room No....

Page 2: this gives you an uncluttered view of your topics and timing, which you may still need to adjust as the detailed preparation gets under way. But at least you'll be able to see what you're doing!

Northern Hemisphere Lettuce
Produce & Seed-Crop Failure

Presentation Timing

2.00 – 2.10	:	Opening & Objective
2.10 – 3.15	:	Agenda Items 1–4
3.15 – 3.30	:	Refreshment Break
3.30 – 5.05	:	Agenda Items 5–8
5.05 – 5.15	:	Presentation Summary
5.15 – 5.20	:	Recommendation
5.20 – 5.50	:	Questions/Discussion
5.50 – 5.55	:	Summary/Close

/2

A presenter of genuine compassion might consider the possibility of further refreshment, about half past five. With discussion under way, the arrival of your secretary discreetly checking the preference of each of the audience members for coffee, tea or something stronger, would no doubt be most welcome.

Page 3: this is nothing more than a simple list of those details you will need to cover during the brief, settling-down period before you really get going with your presentation. If you write them down, you won't forget them.

Opening

Courtesies:	Greetings.
Acknowledgement:	All present/ready to begin.
Logistics:	Presentation time is about 3½ hours, including time for discussion.
	Break at about 3.15.
	Presentation will include many figures (inventory estimates and others). All will be supplied in document at end of presentation.
Subject:	Northern Hemisphere Lettuce: Produce and Seed-Crop Failure.
Questions:	No doubt many. These allowed for at end of various agenda points, and at conclusion of presentation.

/3

As other organisational points occur to you, you simply add them to your list during your preparation.

Page 4: this is where the real action begins. In this case there's a handy and brief anecdote which provides a very comfortable lead-in to the Objective, and this is how it goes:

Anecdote/Objective

In thinking about the opportunity that the northern lettuce failure has presented to us, I remembered a comment made by the famous author, Anthony Trollope, following his visit to Australia many years ago. On his return to England he wrote:
'Australians are second to none—in their own opinion!'

He may not have meant that too kindly. But had he been talking about our lettuce crop-seeds he would have been absolutely right.

Our seeds *are* indeed second to none in their variety, yield and resilience. Furthermore, they can be available in such quantities that today I am going to ask you to:

**Agree to
supply the needs of the
Northern Hemisphere
for the coming season**

/4

That ought to get them in the right frame of mind!

Pages 5 and 6: this is your full, working Agenda, soon to become the very heart of your presentation preparation. As you develop your material it's still possible for you to add, drop or shift various details. For any long, complex presentation, a well set out Agenda is a presenter's best friend.

Agenda

2.10   1.   Northern Hemisphere/Overview
                —Extent of disaster
                —Climatic predictions
                —Duration of seed shortfall

2.20   2.   Company inventory x variety
                —In stock
                —Planned crop yields
                —Estimated surplus
                —Summary

2.35   3.   Varieties(6) x NH suitability
                —Areas
                —Growth rates
                —Resilience/stability
                —Yields/produce crops & seeds
                —Summary

2.55   4.   International distribution
                —Wholesalers/Co-operatives
                —Commercial distributors
                —Government agencies
                —Freighting methods
                —Customs and quarantine
                —Summary
3.15   Break

(Continued . . .)

/5

(Continued)

3.40	5.	Export plan: current surplus

3.40   6.   Export plans(3): increased yields
—Planting schedule
—Contract growers
—Estimated yields
—Harvesting/treatment
—Packaging/languages
—Cost estimates/prices & profit
—Summary

4.20   7.   Unresolved issues
—Competitive activity
—Government support/subsidies
—Aid programmes
—Air charters
—Short-term produce export
—Summary

4.50   8.   Export plans: personnel/logistics
—Management/staff
—Secondments/hirings
—Premises/services
—Summary

5.05   Presentation Summary

5.15   Recommendation (see next page)

/6

Your Presentation Summary should be prepared in full. It represents your conclusions from all that has gone before, and provides the jump-off point for your final Recommendation, the moment when you 'ask for the order'.

Page 7: Just as you prepared the review of your audience, so you can also prepare the presentation Summary and your own Recommendation. It's more good practice for you.

Let me suggest, however, that there are a couple of things for you to consider. Firstly, in only a fortnight, it's a miracle that you got this far. However, it is evident in the Agenda that there are many details to be checked out and a number of important issues to be resolved—areas in which you have had neither the time, the assistance nor the expertise to find all the answers.

Secondly, if there ever was (and I suspect there may have been) any kind of fuzzy managerial notion that one person could handle a global opportunity on this scale, then they've got a hole in their head or their head in a hole!

You can do it yourself, if you like. For *my* part I'd go looking for a helping hand—and after a much more politely put version of the above comments, I would ask the group to consider the Recommendations opposite.

And for an eloquent conclusion, I would then add:

Assuming that our best estimates are confirmed, and that there are no significant problems we think we cannot solve, we should then be in a position to prepare detailed plans which will allow us to:

> **Supply the needs of the Northern Hemisphere for the coming season, and beyond**

All that now remains is for Discussion, followed by your Summary and then your Close.

If perhaps you feel that such detailed planning for a long presentation may have been a bit fussy and long-winded, let me remind you that you're going to spend several hours in intense concentration, and you're going to need all the help you can get! The more care you take at the beginning, the greater will be your satisfaction and reward at the end.

Recommendations

- Approve the maximum
  yield plan in principle

- Form a small task force
  immediately, to:

1. Check all projections
2. Clarify unresolved issues
3. Report in 10 working days

That's about all I can tell you about following a format when planning short or long presentations, and all the lengths in between, and we'll leave the subject with one, final thought.

When you know the rules you can soon learn how to bend them, how to take the short cuts, but if you don't know the rules, then beware. In a maze most will lose their way!

VI

Presentation
preparation

24
Step-by-step preparation

By the time you've completed the hard thinking which gets you to your Objective, your Agenda and your Recommendation, most of the really tough going is behind you. You know exactly where you are heading. Now all you have to do is complete your plan of how to get there.

The three categories of content preparation for any presentation are:

1. What are you going to *say?*
2. What are you going to *show?*
3. What are you going to *give?*

With experience, all three can be decided upon almost simultaneously and your task now is to complete your step-by-step preparation in a natural and comfortable sequence.

What are you going to say?

Working from the headlines of your Agenda, you must now decide exactly what you want to say in support of each point, which details you want to include, and what style of language will be the clearest and most persuasive for your audience.

There are two basic options for this part of your preparation, the Key Point Option and the Script Option. Which you select will depend partly on the complexity of your presentation, and partly on your own level of experience and confidence.

Presenting from key points

For some of you the simple notation of Key Points in sequence for each Agenda item will be sufficient. If your Agenda is brief and straight-forward, if you are thoroughly confident about your knowledge of your subject and about your ability to be lucid and if you are not

113

intimidated by your audience, then this can be a highly successful technique.

As you work through your 'what to say' preparation, you will note these key points down, with the intention of using them for your rehearsals and, later, of taking them with you into the presentation itself. (Failure to do so may suggest a strong urge to self-destruct. In the excitement of the moment, without your notes you may accidentally miss an important step in the development of your presentation argument and once you are past that point it can be difficult to go back. Your notes are your security blanket and no one will think the less of you for having them there, assuming that they notice them at all.)

Because you will (please) rehearse thoroughly, this simple method of using key points can be highly effective. It is certainly more economical of your time than attempting to script your presentation in full. It is equally effective in helping you to decide where you wish to use visual aids or present products or ideas, and in spotting where you will need to provide special data for the consideration of your audience.

Scripting a presentation

So far, so good. Let's now look at the Script Option, which is to prepare your presentation notes in full, writing down *exactly* what you want to say for each Agenda point and how you want to say it.

Although time-consuming, this method has several advantages. For example:

- Where it is important for you to choose your words with great care for a particular topic or audience, it ensures that you do so.

- Irrelevancies can sometimes sneak into a presentation delivered from points, sometimes as after-thoughts, and often because we never know when to stop talking! Scripting allows you to spot any bits of nonsense which may have crept in and edit them out.

- Your script and your first rehearsal will help you check your timing more accurately than with the Key Point option, and if you are running over time you will be able to see where you need to do some pruning.

- A script can be a valuable confidence builder, particularly if you are feeling a bit shaky about the forthcoming event. By the time you've completed your full presentation script, you will have put so much thought and effort into it, the chances of you fluffing it on the day will be small.

A word of caution. If you are going to script your presentation in full, do not confuse this with writing a document. The big trick is making sure that you write as you speak, using your own individual style. Then, if you do spot some lumpy bits of business language, you can cross them out right away. If you don't normally say that, don't write it down.

There's nothing so disconcerting as listening to a normally cheerful, intelligent soul using ill-fitting language, making their presentation with all the joyless solemnity of a talking Annual Report.

Being solemn does not make you more believable. Being serious does not mean you have to be po-faced dull. It's perfectly possible to be deadly serious about your subject, yet relaxed and pleasant in the manner in which you present it. You will achieve this when you use language which is simple and clear and natural to *you*.

Having prepared your script it is then quite simple to highlight important thoughts or phrases. After several rehearsals you may find you have gained sufficient confidence to cut back to key points only for the presentation itself.

I use both methods, and sometimes a mixture of the two. For a topic with which I'm very familiar I'll work from Key Points only, and sometimes from Agenda points only if each is pretty much on one topic.

For presentations where absolute clarity is called for, where accidental detours are to be avoided, where timing is critical, where reasoned argument needs to build to careful conclusion, then I favour scripting. It takes longer to prepare, but in my view the results always justify the effort.

Presentations which require scripting will always be in the minority. Most that you will make will be within the familiar category, so we're not talking about a life's work ahead of you!

Scripting your presentation can be rather fun. Remember, no one's going to see your script but you, and you'll be writing the way you speak. You certainly don't have to worry about perfect syntax and the finer points of punctuation. A dash here and a slash there will be just fine. Certainly you will have no intention of reading your script word for word, so you can take lots of short cuts. In your rehearsals you will practice until you can comfortably look at your audience, glancing at your notes only as you need to from time to time.

Using notes

Now, what about notes? Always providing that you do not intend to use them as a full life-support system, my advice would be 'don't leave home without them'. I have never made a major presentation without notes, nor has anyone I know, so why should you?

Only a tiny minority of presenters are so bold or so skilled that they can carry a complex presentation without any assistance. And how unaided are they really?

To start with, many will have produced an Agenda for the benefit of their audience, and will be working from a copy of that themselves. Some will use visual aids (which we'll come to in a moment), slides or overheads which summarise the very points about which they are speaking, and we could call these notes by any other name. If you look very closely you will often see the seemingly unaided presenter discreetly place a small key point reminder note somewhere close by.

In days gone by the expression 'off the cuff' was no idle phrase—after all, where better to glance for the odd reminder? Before we all stopped smoking, cigarette packets were often used as sneaky mini-note pads, and the most cunningly concealed notes I ever noticed were written by a colleague on the palm of his left hand!

I really find all that furtive and rather foolish, and for good presentation notes the answer lies somewhere between the exotic extremes and a horrid heap of dog-eared paper. I favour having points or notes clearly typed and then marked or highlighted as necessary, but you will decide what suits you best.

The only golden rule is that neatness counts, with clarity running a very close second. Not being able to find your place will be worse than having no notes at all!

What are you going to show?

As you prepare your presentation notes it will become apparent where you may need to use a visual aid or wish to demonstrate an item, in order to focus audience attention or make a dramatic point.

As these thoughts occur to you, all you need to do at this stage is to make a one-word notation (say in the right-hand margin of your notes) and when your notes are complete you simply return to this column and review your decisions.

Now you will decide if you've picked the right ones and put them in the right place. If it's then obvious that some of these items are going to take a bit of finding or preparing, you have plenty of time to get organised and thus avoid last-minute calamities.

For example, if you want to show an area development map which, in its existing form, is too complex to use, then for it to be of any real value you will have to get it simplified. This will take a little time.

If you want to reveal a competitive product display in your presentation it's unlikely you'll be able to get your hands on this overnight. Someone is going to need a bit of warning.

Warehouses can be notoriously slow in supplying product in quantity, if that is what you want. So if you wish to avoid buying at retail prices at the last minute, you'd better let someone know what you need and by when.

The preparation of visual aids (charts, slides and overheads) is a world of its own, and we will deal with those in a later chapter.

The point is that you must make your 'what to show' decisions early, if indeed you are going to show anything at all.

Many will tell you that a presentation should *always* be punctuated with visual aids and such, quoting 'seeing is believing' and other Confucian-sounding truths.

I don't altogether agree with that and have often watched in dismay as those who take the thought too literally fade into obscurity in their own presentations. By over-using visual aids, they become shadowy presences, voices in the dimness chanting their messages from one image to the next. Leaning on their visual crutches they lose centre-stage and with it both their credibility and their ability to persuade. The data are left to do the persuading, not the presenters.

When you are considering 'what to show', I would suggest that you use visual aids not because you think you have to, but because you know you want to. Then you will become much more selective in your choice of material. With this rule-of-economy, each visual aid that you do choose will then become more distinctive (and useful) than if it were merely one of a herd.

There will also always be presentations that you can make without the aid of any visual aids whatsoever. When your Objective is defined and when your purpose is clear, do not be afraid to take on your task *without* the benefit of visual crutches. Remember, *you* are your best visual aid, and sometimes 'what to show' need only be your thinking, your conviction and yourself.

What are you going to give?

You can whiz through your 'what to give' decisions just as quickly as you can memorise the 3-G Giving Formula—Guidance, Guff and Goodies. Got that? Right! Let's take them each in turn, and using more dignified language let us first translate them into:

Guidance: Your Agenda

Guff: Documentation

Goodies: Samples and/or souvenirs

Guiding your audience

Giving guidance to your audience is simply a matter of outlining your Agenda before you begin to work through your presentation point by point.

You can do this verbally only, or with a visual aid, in your opening remarks, or preferably immediately following the statement of your Objective.

You can put it in writing and provide a typed copy of the Agenda for each member of the audience. This can either be placed in position where the members of your audience will sit when they arrive or, if you are the visitor, distributed by you as you prepare to get started.

I favour the latter method, the provision of a typed Agenda, plus a commentary from the presenter such as: 'As you can see from your Agenda, we are going to cover . . .' and you simply read through your Agenda headings. This allows the audience members to have a good look at where you're heading, which will often heighten their anticipation and will certainly help to settle everyone down.

So for guidance, provision of an Agenda is your task, and you must be sure this is ready in the form you require it before your presentation. Now let us turn to guff, or documentation.

Documents and details

As we have seen in the presentation examples, it is frequently wise to provide information for your audience members to read and consider when your presentation is over. Often this will be in a lot more detail than you will have covered, as you will have extracted and used only strictly relevant facts and figures.

As you work through your presentation notes it will quickly become evident where the supply of documentation is called for, and to what extent. So, you make a note of this as you go and then later decide how you wish to 'package' this for your audience members. (The more professionally this is done, the better it will reflect on you and your organisation.)

By the way, when it comes to the quantities of your guidance and guff, *always* have extra copies of both your Agenda and your document. You seldom can be quite sure that extra people will not be present unexpectedly. Without an agenda for reference they're going to have a miserable time peeping over other people's shoulders and will feel decidedly second-class departing without their own copies.

Spare copies hardly ever need go to waste. If you still have some left over you can always repeat your presentation to your staff, or to colleagues who might be very interested to know what you've been up to.

Samples and souvenirs

Finally, we turn to goodies—samples of materials or products you wish to give to each audience member, and any other souvenirs of your presentation which will add to its impact and memorability.

As we have seen in 'what to show', obtaining products can be a lengthy business, so the sooner you decide and order, the better. Always remember, your delivery date should be several days before your presentation. Twittering that you would have liked your audience to have a sample but 'they haven't arrived' or 'were out of stock' is not at all impressive and smacks of serious disorganisation.

Giving souvenirs, stamping a memory on the minds of your audience is not a must, it's an option. But often it can be done at very little cost and with great effect, and is well worth a moment's thought.

In our Dog Deodorant presentation, the example of the dog bone souvenir would surely have been remembered by the members of the audience—at least for as long as it took them to agree to the Recommendation! The memories of some souvenirs can last a lot longer than that.

At one conference I attended, two-person client-agency teams had gathered from all over the world to present their most recent advertising campaigns and to review their future plans. The Canadians were outstanding. Their work was witty and wonderful, and the client and agency representatives obviously had a top working relationship.

At the end of his presentation, the Canadian speaker, with justifiable pleasure, declared: 'We're proud of the work we do. And it gets done well because we work and play and fight as a team. And to remind you all of the benefits of good teamwork in the days to come, we would like you all to accept this small souvenir.' Whereupon he gave each of the delegates a hockey puck. A simple, inexpensive Canadian hockey puck, which said it all.

The puck has sat on my desk from that day to this, a constant reminder that good teamwork matters, and forever providing a warm memory of some very smart Canadians.

On another occasion, for even less cost, I borrowed an idea from a sales friend and zoomed off to another conference, this time on the subject of 'How to do business with Government'. Although conspicuously junior to the other delegates, I got asked because I happened to have helped obtain some government business in our area, and on that basis, I suppose, they felt they could hardly leave me at home. Good for them!

The presentations went by, long on earnestness and short on results and finally it was my turn. With as much modesty as I could muster I told our story of persistent pursuit and ultimate success, paused, and then continued:

Ladies and gentlemen, I would now like to bring you a special *message on behalf of my colleagues and myself. Before I do so, however, would you all please rise?*

Another pause, while they clambered to their feet, all looking distinctly puzzled and, as one delegate told me later, dismayed at the thought that I might be about to say prayers!

Ladies and gentlemen, would each of you now please look under the seat of your chair, and tell me if you find anything.

After some rather awkward encounters with the furniture, three delegates produced one-dollar bills I had taped there before the presentation—each as pleased as a child who'd found a treasure.

Well, ladies and gentlemen, that is our message. Quite simply, you've got to get off your arse to earn a buck!

Now, this may be an old-hat joke these days, but it was new then, and after a moment of stunned surprise they were all hooting with laughter. The message was sharp and clear. Those who got moving got business. Whenever I meet any of those folk today, they still laugh and reminisce about the time the kid from nowhere taught them all a lesson—with no hard feelings, and all for just three dollars.

Somewhere, at the beginning of all this, I remember suggesting that while presentations are certainly hard work, there's no reason why they can't be fun too. A smile and a joke relieves the tension for us all, and where better to do this than at the end? What better way to leave your audience than with the memory of the time you cared enough to give them a first-rate presentation, and dared enough to make them laugh?

25
Preparation example and check lists

As you make more and more presentations, you may develop your own check-listing methods. Until then here's an example to get you started, based on the step-by-step preparation we have discussed in the previous chapter, and using another imaginary situation for demonstration purposes.

The 'Dream home estate' development

This time you can be a young, energetic property developer. You own a big chunk of land in the right place, and you have plans to create an estate of twenty individual, high quality four bedroom family homes, with all the trimmings.

Your plans have been drawn up by professional civil engineers and architects. Your development and construction costs have been calculated by your team of builders, quantity surveyors, pool designers, landscape gardeners and goodness knows who else, and you have solid estimates (plus or minus ten per cent) of what it's going to cost, right down to popping in the last petunia.

Good stuff, but you need funds. You have a third of the money but you want the bank to put up the rest over a two year period, because that's where you know you can get the best rate of interest. You make a one hour appointment with your bankers, make a note to get your hair trimmed and your solid-citizen suit cleaned and pressed, and settle down to prepare your thirty minute presentation, with another thirty minutes set aside for post-presentation discussion.

Your Objective is crystal clear, your Proposal/Recommendation reflects your Objective (both of which include the actual amount you want to borrow), and you have decided that your Agenda will cover:

1. Estate location
2. Estate ground plan
3. Proposed dwellings/architects' designs
4. Construction schedule
5. Pre-completion promotion and sales plan
6. Cost estimates

And you intend to Summarise at the end of your Agenda.

With this Agenda you've set yourself six items to cover in a little under thirty minutes, an average of about five minutes each.

Right away that tells you that you've no time to dawdle, but on the other hand you know you'd be ill-advised to blitz your bankers with a high-pressure sales pitch. A steady, business-like presentation is called for here. You know your subject inside out, decide to work from key points, and this is how your check lists evolve:

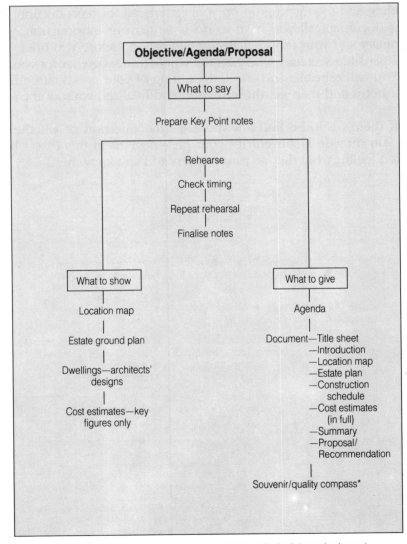

* To show the way to the new estate—and to a new standard of high quality, family home development.

Isn't that easy! Now you can see at a glance exactly what you have to do.

To illuminate your presentation you know that you are going to need four visuals (or a few more if you want to show the variation of home designs in greater splendour). Your next step is to extract the key figures you want to use in your discussion of cost estimates, and then you are ready to have your visuals prepared.

For distribution to your audience your Agenda only needs a proper heading and then typing up on your letterhead for reproduction. For your document all you have to do is write your introduction, your Summary and your Proposal/Recommendation, before you brief your indispensible secretary who puts the whole thing together for you.

You will rehearse and check the timing of your presentation from your notes and then get those revised and finalised without the least bother.

If there's a loose end anywhere it's the question of whether or not you provide a souvenir of your presentation. In this case I have mixed feelings, but they're *your* bankers and you know best!

26

Presenting with colleagues

Once upon a time, in a moment of shining truth, a man called Murphy voiced his immutable law: 'If it can go wrong, it will.'

I have a strong suspicion that Murphy made presentations for a living, wasn't very good at it, never checked anything and, above all, was an absolute dead loss when it came to communicating with others, which is, of course, vital whenever you are presenting with colleagues.

Often you will make presentations on your own, but on many occasions you will make them in partnership or as one of a team, and whenever this occurs the malevolent Murphy is going to be out there waiting for you.

To side-step this unhappy prospect you will have to deal with the need for early discussion and agreement (of your mutual presentation intentions and format) and then, as far as you are able, ensure that everyone is fully prepared and rehearsed.

Then you will still have to face what can sometimes be the biggest challenge of all—simply getting everyone together in the right place at the right time—and your world and mine is full of the tales of times when *that* went wrong!

So, any time you are making a presentation with one or more of your colleagues, let me suggest another law to live by: 'There's no such thing as a walk-up start.' If you've any hope of getting it right, you must have clear communication and understanding between each other in advance of the event.

Why more than one presenter?

Other than the rather dotty decision to 'break up' a presentation by providing a variety of presenters for variety's sake, the real answer is that where an agenda includes areas of specialty, it should be true that each can best be presented by the acknowledged expert.

So, for a proposal to improve the efficiency of a mining operation, different experts in turn may review geological indications, future production levels, environmental impact, and the likely reaction of unions to change. Or, on a jollier note, for the new yacht on your shopping list, the hull design may be presented by one expert and the sail plan by another.

This is broadly speaking as it should be, but there are exceptions and there are options. The exceptions to the expert-as-presenter-rule rest in the matters of talent and time.

For example, if your expert has absolutely no presentation ability, or perhaps so thick an accent that few will understand him or her, then another way will have to be found.

On the question of time, if your presentation is so brief that bringing in a number of experts to present for only a moment each will appear absurd, alternatives must be considered.

Solving these problems calls for honest assessment, good management, and considerable diplomacy!

Your talent options with awful-but-expert presenters are to work and rehearse with them until they improve sufficiently to make the team or, failing that, to persuade them to attend the presentation but let another person do the talking. That person could be you, or another member of their department.

A further option is for you to volunteer to make the expert's headline point and then quickly open up the subject for discussion. Frequently experts who are dreadful presenters are quite wonderful when it comes to questions, answers and comments. So, leading yourself and then deferring to the expert can often be a very satisfactory and harmonious alternative.

Your time options are to amend your agenda and reduce the number of requisite experts, if that is possible, or, if you simply must have the experts handle their own specialties, then you may have to renegotiate the overall length of the presentation, so that the impression of unseemly haste and confusion is avoided.

These are really matters of practicality and common sense. However, such decisions cannot be left to the last minute, and forward planning is the key.

Providing you are well organised, making presentations with colleagues can be a great experience. To start with you are not alone. You are sharing in an enterprise, and you will have many memories to recall in days to come—of the wounds that healed along the way, of the strides you took together, and even though you often doubted it would happen, of the moment when together you got it right!

Before we reach that euphoric state, let's just take a closer look to see who's dancing, who's leading, and what steps there are to learn that might be helpful.

Choosing a partner

The simplest combination is the double act. These come in a number of varieties, and your choice of pairing will depend on how you assess your audience and the degree of difficulty you think you may have in achieving your objective.

Senior partners

One possibility is that you may need a partner to be Senior but Silent. When you are clearly the right person to make the presentation but know you will be out-ranked by some members of your audience who are touchy about such matters, then you should ask a senior colleague to accompany you. This is not lack of courage. It's common sense.

You do all the work, you make sure your senior partner is fully briefed and you still make the entire presentation. Your colleague is there to look wise, be supportive, to flatter the audience with his or her presence, and to participate fully in discussions and decisions.

When discussion occurs, sometimes higher ranking members of your audience will prefer to chat with your senior partner rather than yourself. This is no time to get bitter and twisted. That's why you brought your partner along, and achieving your Objective is more important than worrying about your tender feelings. Look ahead. If your presentation is successful *you* may be invited on your own next time!

Junior partners

At the other end of the pecking order there will be times when you will need to be partnered by your Indispensable Junior, to help you with the physical aspects of your presentation. His or her silent assistance may range from the swift distribution of items, to the on-cue operation of equipment or the timely circulation of the coffee pot.

Neither of you should regard such tasks as menial, for they can be very necessary to the smooth conduct of a presentation. You should, of course, include your junior in your rehearsals, so that he or she understands exactly what you want done and when, why you need it, and why—on this occasion—you prefer your junior to remain mostly mute. (It's part of his or her training, and his or her turn will surely come. But not this time!)

Equal partners

With those exceptions, Full Partnerships are the more usual combination, with both parties making a more or less equal contribution to the presentation. For the very reason that you will usually have complete confidence and trust in your equal partner, this should be the occasion for special vigilance.

Taking each other comfortably for granted has been known to lead to hideous hullabaloo on the highway as one or the other cries, 'I thought *you* were bringing that!'

Even worse, presentations launched without careful prior consultation have sometimes produced rather dangerous dialogue. Presenter A makes a point. Presenter B (hitherto the great companion and faithful ally) awakens to mutter, 'I didn't know you were going to say *that*!' and promptly embarks on a line of argument for which A was totally unprepared.

Stumbling into an encounter session in front of your audience is unlikely to yield the result you were seeking. If you are going to agree to disagree and present different points of view, that may be fine but do make sure you plan to do so well before the presentation, not during it!

The team presentation

Any difficulties of organisation you may encounter in preparing for a partnership presentation will increase in direct proportion to the number of participants in a Team Presentation—which is a well established sub-section of Murphy's Law.

To start with, the attitudes of the selected team members will range all the way from confident enthusiasm to deep apprehension. At first most will have somewhat misty views of how the presentation is to be conducted and what is to be their contribution to it. Sorting this lot out *early* is essential. Good communication and rehearsals are the keys, and procedure should include at least the following four steps:

1. *Team briefing.* This should be conducted in a meeting with all present, and should include the presentation Objective, draft Agenda, and approximate timing. The object of the briefing is to make sure everyone has the same basic details right at the start, to obtain the team's understanding and approval of the Objective, and to review the Agenda—which may very well benefit from any suggested adjustment.

   This is where team leaders may have to tread the tricky path between democracy and autocracy. After all, they have to get it done, but they want the full co-operation of all the participants along the way. Bullying the team members is certainly not recommended. Open discussion and enthusiasm is.

   The team departs from the briefing, each to prepare, and with a series of dates recorded for the next steps, the first of which is a review of progress.

2. *Progress review.* For this each must come prepared to outline the content of his or her segment of the presentation, and to indicate requirements for such things as equipment, visual aids, displays and so forth. Then, if these items are needed, decisions can be taken whether they are to be co-ordinated or procured independently.

3. *First rehearsal.* This is usually a very untidy event, with presenters at very different levels of readiness, and so needs to be handled

with considerable good humour, patience and honest encouragement. Tightly pursed lips and indications of displeasure will
not help matters. The leader can do that privately, if it's called
for—or, better still, privately offer help to those in need.

4. *Dress rehearsal.* For the full dress rehearsal everyone and
everything should be ready. If possible, it should take place
in the same venue in which the presentation is planned, so
that all can 'feel' the room and become thoroughly familiar with
their surroundings and the facilities.

Each presenter will take his or her place in turn, changeovers
from one to the next will be cued and smoothed and each
segment of the presentation rehearsed for as long as it takes
to get it right.

These four steps are the minimum necessary for a good team
presentation. The briefing and progress review meetings need not
be lengthy, but those who undertake team presentations without
rehearsals do so at their peril, facing the near certainty of patchy and
unpersuasive performance.

On the other hand, the clear impression of mutual confidence
and unity of purpose will be made when a team presentation has
been put together in close consultation and has then been well
rehearsed. This has a positive impact on the audience. When an
audience sees a team that works well together, they will see a team
that can work well with them.

Getting well organised

Arriving at this happy state will not always be easy. Amongst those
who have not known the pleasure of completing a successful team
presentation, there will be those who may be testy about attending
meetings, touchy about rehearsals, resistant to togetherness, and
reluctant to prepare. The shy will be elusive. The bold and busy even
more so. Getting their full co-operation and the best each has to give
is the job of whoever is the leader.

Often that will be you. When it's your turn, how you demonstrate
your team leadership will depend on your own experience and style,
and sometimes on your level of seniority.

However, whether you are the instigator of the presentation or
have been delegated to organise it, your responsibilities are the same.
Whatever you are called—co-ordinator, manager, leader—should make
no difference whatsoever. Fretting about your lowly rank (if that's

your problem) will not change matters and will be quite irrelevant. Providing you know what you're doing, it will have little bearing on whether or not you can get the job done.

For good team presentation leadership, once again it's time to think of others. What do the others on the team need, how can you help them, how can you encourage them and even reward them— all without being pushy or a pest?

Organising a team presentation is not the time to be play-acting leader and issuing terse orders. It's time for clear thinking and friendly persuasion. The best all-round formula I can offer you is a mix in equal parts of unbounded energy, firm resolution, a sharp eye for detail and a generous spirit, which can exist in us all, regardless of the rung we stand on.

The making of memories

Presenting with colleagues can be tremendous fun and, serious purpose aside, can often be a source of comedy, drama and reward.

My favourite lunatic episode was the Case of the Lost Partner, which occurred when two of our senior colleagues were invited to England to make a presentation on the subject of 'Creativity'. They were asked to present to a group of managers attending a high-powered residential course outside London. They were staying in town, and had to arrive at the country seat of learning in time to start their presentation at 10.00 am.

They did a great double-act, these two—very pointed, marvellously eccentric and entertaining—but because of their propensity to lose things on the way to the start were seldom let out without a keeper. On this occasion, however, a keeper was deemed an unnecessary expense—and no one dreamt for a moment that they could possibly lose each other!

A little late off the mark, slightly fogged by jet lag, and struggling with a motley collection of tapes, slides and visual aids, they headed for the nearest Underground station. Tickets procured, they were juggling the goods between them, when their train tore into the station with the most unnerving roar.

The more agile of the two, who happened to know where he was going, leapt aboard as the doors opened. His partner, still wrestling with his assorted bundles, innocent of his exact destination but with the tickets tucked firmly in his hat, was cut off by a rampaging herd of commuters and missed his chance. The doors zomped shut. As the train gathered speed the two could be seen scampering down

the carriage and the platform respectively, bellowing at each other in unison, 'Catch the next train to Whurble-Burble', and 'Where? Where did you say?' And so they parted.

Confident that his slow-footed companion would soon catch up, our agile presenter proceeded. An hour's delay at the course, and no Slow Foot. So an hour late, absent friend and missing aids notwith-standing, there was nothing for it but to begin. Laying off for the mislaid bits and bravely playing both parts, Agile was well under way when the conference room doors were flung open.

Minus his hat, but otherwise unperturbed, in dashed Slow Foot. 'Don't worry, dear boy', he cried, with consummate irrelevance. 'I've still got the tickets!'

All everyone could do was laugh and after a moment of reunion, more laughter and a cup of tea, they all went back to the beginning and started over again. Which just goes to show that there's hardly ever a problem that can't be overcome by the combination of good humour and good will.

I will treasure always a memory of a really tough team presentation— not simply for the fact that it got done, but for the contributions made by so many, for the sense of excitement that grew as the job took shape, and for the delight when it was over and successful and all stood proud and tall.

It was a beast—a huge product launch, an audience of a hundred and fifty guests, off-shore, an hour-and-a-half, six presenters and the demand for both triple-screen excitement to match the moment *and* triple-A security for obvious reasons.

Such events are not whipped up over the weekend and this one was more than six months in the making. Most of the presenters were relatively inexperienced, certainly for a presentation on this scale, and all had to be coaxed into unfamiliar scripting and asked to indicate their needs for slides and other material well in advance. If that wasn't bad enough, they had to be fitted for their presentation wardrobes, and rehearsed until word perfect.

We did have our moments along the way, but in the end six presenters didn't miss a single beat. Nine hundred slides appeared on cue, miles of tape rolled on time and we finished with just thirty seconds to spare on the clock. This was all as it should have been after such intense preparation, and to the technicians that was almost reward enough.

However, what really counted was the moment the audience rose as one and cheered them to the echo. That was when they really knew they had done well. *That* was pay day. One day, presenting with your colleagues, I hope you too will know as fine a moment.

27
Visual aids

In several previous chapters there have been various comments and cautions about visual aids and now the time has come to look at these more closely.

You will already have a storehouse of information on the subject. After all, in one form or another you've been exposed to show-and-tell ever since your first days at pre-school, but now we are grown up people (who make presentations), and it's time to really focus on the purposes and types of visual aids, to consider questions of choice, preparation and handling and sometimes to count the cost.

Before we get to all that, however, let's be quite sure we know what is meant by 'visual aid', both obviously and when we apply a little imagination.

What is a visual aid?

In the context of presentations, clearly it is any object or visual message which helps in the communication of our information or ideas.

By far the great majority of visual aids (VAs) contain words or numbers and we will return to these in a moment. First I want to drag 'objects' into the discussion, simply because too often they're over-looked.

Bringing messages to life

Objects can include all kinds of props, and these can often make their point with more visual impact and memorability than any collection of neatly rendered messages. They must, however, be selected with a sharp eye for relevance on the one hand and the potential for distraction on the other.

Let us imagine, for example, that you are presenting label designs for a new brand of lusty Caribbean rum, targetted to macho men, and strong on the imagery of the pirate doings of days gone by. You can present your designs in the tidy and time-honoured way, one by one, leading to your recommended design complete with eye-

patched pirate and his disreputable parrot. There's nothing wrong with that.

To make a more dramatic impact—and if you were completely out of your mind—you might consider presenting your designs with a parrot on your own shoulder. However, the prospects for distraction, a costly dry-cleaning bill and lacerations of the ear lobe are almost unbounded.

Stepping back from the brink of that insanity, however, there is another idea—the real thing. As you reach the peak of your design presentation, whoosh, you reveal your pirate and his parrot—your muscular, bearded model in full costume, complete with cutlass, feathered friend, a gleam in his one good eye, and a thirst that only sailors know.

Never mind how *you* feel about this manifestation! Consider the effect of these 'props' on your audience, and give them credit for having a little imagination. Your somewhat predictable label design has come to life before their very eyes, and visions of huge posters, exciting commercials and a knock-out sales conference in a warm climate are zinging through their minds without any prompting from you.

That's what you can achieve with a well chosen visual aid, an object which stamps your intentions more powerfully than any little label or a thousand words could ever do.

Whenever you feel the need for visual dramatisation of a headline or any part of your presentation, the real limits lie only within your own imagination. Sometimes budget may also play a part in this, but visual impact need not always be costly and to demonstrate this, let's look at another, very simple example of how to bring a conventional visual aid to life.

Jazzing an agenda

This time let us imagine your agenda has just two points prior to your Recommendation, namely the advantages and disadvantages of your proposal, or in language we all use every day, the Good News and the Bad News. You want to signal your points with a visual aid— a chart, an overhead slide or a flip-board.

You have two choices: the predictable or the visual. Conventionally (and assuming 'Good News/Bad News' is language appropriate to your audience) your message will be revealed to read:

Proposal: Xxxxxx xx xxxxxxxx

Agenda

1. The Good News
2. The Bad News
3. Recommendation

With a touch of imagination, however, this can come to life if your ready-for-use message reveals only what is indicated on the top visual aid opposite.

Then as you announce your agenda points, with a thick felt pen you boldly add the symbols that we all understand so well (as shown opposite).

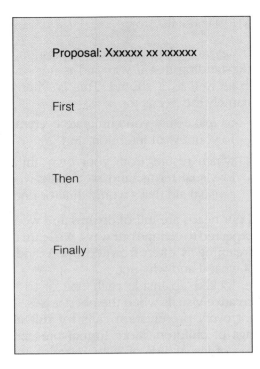

You state your Proposal, then add: 'There are only three items for us to consider, the advantages, the dis-advantages and the solution. Taking these in turn, we will look

first (draw in happy face) at the Good News . . .

then (draw in sad face) the Bad News, and . . .

finally (big, bold tick) we will present our Recommendation!'

Which now brings us back to the original question, what is a visual aid, and the understanding that if your aid is not strongly *visual* it's not doing its job as well as it should. This is where two important factors emerge, namely the needs for:

1. Discipline—to make sure you eliminate everything superfluous to your visual intention, and

2. Creativity — which results from your own ability to see ideas in visual terms, and so decide whether you have a visual aid that's worthwhile or not!

In childhood our heads are full of dreams and wonder. Then, little by little, we are expected to change our ways. We learn that the peaceful pursuit of day-dreaming is often frowned upon, and slowly we can lose the magic of what-if and why-not.

It's still there, locked up inside each one of us and any one of you can evolve creative visuals when the need arises.

Of course, not every presentation calls for ruffian pirates or the sunshine drawings of children. More formal presentations may call for the production of visual aids of style, restraint and elegance, but these too are creative decisions you will have to reach according to your subject, your audience and, above all, the purpose you intend them to serve.

Why use visual aids?

Visual aids are used in most well organised presentations in order to help the presenters communicate their messages clearly to all the members of the audience, and so help the audience fully understand both detail and direction.

Visual aids should not be flung into a presentation just for the sake of it but for specific purposes, the chief of which are:

Clarity: Your Proposal, Recommendation and any other key points will be expressed in terms identical to all, and thus lessen the possibility of misinterpretation of what you have said. Also, if you use a visual aid for your Agenda or any other sequence information, everyone will be able to see your 'map', the direction you intend to take and the territory you intend to cover.

Simplicity: Complex data or thoughts can be reduced to simple, summarised form. (Busy folk with much on their minds will listen to your dissertations on this and that, but inside each one will be a little voice muttering, 'Okay, okay, but what's the *main* point of all this?' *That's* what you put on your visual aid.

Interest: The intermittent use of visual aids will help you to hold the interest of your audience, whether by direction ('now, think about *this*'), or by summary ('how about that').

Memorability: The better, more graphic your visual aids are, the better your key points will register—and the better your total presentation (and yourself) will be remembered.

Time saving: Well organised, well designed visual aids will help you manage the timing of your presentation—by highlighting the key points and by marking the transition from one point to the next.

Entertainment: While all presentations have serious purpose, many will have moments when you can lighten the load.

Flattery: Good visual aids send unmistakable signals to audiences that you took some trouble with this presentation, you thought out what mattered to *them*, and then expressed it visually and well. The pay-back will be that you will be seen as skilled and professional in your presentation—and presumably in other things too.

So, your basic purposes are to keep your audience informed, wide awake and interested with visual as well as verbal messages and thus help your audience and yourself.

If any one of your visual aids is not visual and it's no help, then by definition it's not a visual aid and needs some serious rethinking.

What kinds are there?

Many—perhaps more than we might at first think when we're a bit new to presentations. Let's have a look at the broad categories that are common today, and then keep an eye open for what will surely become available tomorrow.

Filled space: Charts, designs or pre-lettered data on any surface.

Blank space: For small presentations, those in which a feeling of
spontaneity is called for (or those to which you've
been summoned at the last possible moment), you
can't beat blank space and a fistful of bold-stroke felt
pens. Your blank space may be an easel and scribble
pad, sheets of board, acetate sheets for overhead
projection, wipe-clean boards—even blackboards and
chalk. Your space can be completely blank when you
begin, or you may have pre-lettered some information
which you later add to or deface.

Projection: For which all you need is an idea and another blank
space (wall or screen) to get you started. Then you
can project overhead slides (acetates), mounted slides
(usually 35 mm) and film in a variety of sizes.

Electronics: Videotape in all its wonder, segments and sequences,
moving and still, is an easy way to bring reference
and interest to any presentation at the push of a button.
Sound (not visual, but certainly an optional aid) is
all around us and often over-looked for use in
presentations. It can be used to help settle an audience
with background or theme music, for dramatic effect,
or for demonstration. (Why on earth would you
describe a sound when you can produce it?)

*Props, products
and people:*   Objects, if you like, including live ones!

Which kind and how many visual aids you will choose will obviously
vary from one presentation to another. These decisions will sometimes
hinge on how much time you have to get your visual aids prepared
and what you can afford to spend. The memory of the time I forgot
to ask the price can still make me flinch in painful remembrance.

On this occasion I was asked to make a presentation to the full
head office team of a client, a first of its kind, and indeed it was
something of a compliment to be invited. Over-excited at the prospect
and wishing to do well by both the client and the company, I swept
into full scale production of a set of gleaming 35 mm slides, with
elegant typography and diagrams, each slide resplendent in the client's
colours and complete with the client's logo discreetly placed bottom
right.

Great idea, but . . .! Short on time and long on co-operative workers,
whose mission in life was to achieve the impossible (especially when

you asked them nicely), these glorious slides were produced with record speed and off I dashed to the presentation, oblivious of the cost and having never once thought to ask the dreaded question!

Presentation mission accomplished, some time later I returned to the office to be confronted by an ominous pile of costs pulsating on the in-tray and a quick addition revealed the appalling truth of the bottom line.

I didn't know what to do with the wretched things! Prompt payment was in order, but what to do with the costs? I couldn't charge the client. I hadn't told the accountants what I was up to in the first place, and they took a most unfriendly view of being asked to bury a body of that size.

I recycled the presentation as often as I could get anyone to listen to it, in the forlorn hope that this would somehow help to justify the awesome cost of the visual aids, but the sums folk weren't having any of that—and rightly so!

In the end there was nothing left but to own up and plead for equal measures of write-off and forgiveness, which were duly and generously granted. I had suffered enough! Never again did I ever forget to ask, 'How much is it all going to cost?'

Preparation and briefing

As we have seen, time factors and costs can be real considerations when you are preparing visual aids. However, assuming that you have ample time and money, let's now look at matters of shape and style and the possibilities and the pitfalls of the most commonly used types of visual aids.

The most familiar overall shape used for visual aids is the trusty oblong. This comes in two versions known as portrait and landscape (see p. 142), descriptions which obviously have their origins in the art world.

Looking at these, one realises that the portrait shape is familiar to us from the books, newspapers, reports and correspondence that we *read*. The landscape shape owes its familiarity to things we *see*, movies, television, and the majority of happy snaps we take on our holidays—all visuals!

Despite the comfort we feel in looking at visual images in the landscape format and the great opportunity this shape offers for bold visual messages that can flex their muscles in the wide open space

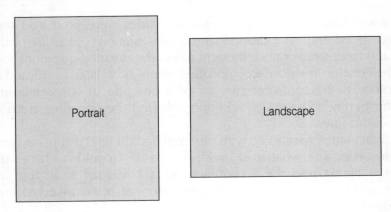

available, there exists a lamentable tendency for presenters to use the portrait shape, often with most uncomfortable results.

Portrait shaped visual aids appear with cramped messages, hunched in their narrow columns of space. When projected onto a conventional screen (which is almost always landscape), inevitably they loose their tops and tails. If acetates, they present the presenter with the problem of slithering the things up and down. If slides—and the projector is actually within reach—then cranking it up and down or shoving telephone books under it are popular but unprofessional options.

So, if you are planning projection, you have your first visual preparation choice to make.

Will it be this?

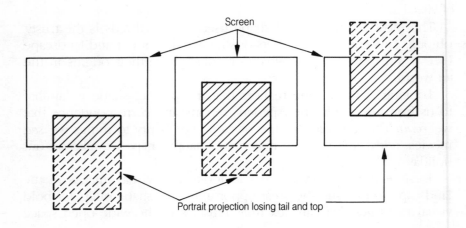

Or will it be this?

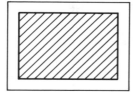

Landscape projection
on landscape screen

The choice between the two shapes often seems to occur by default. Frequently we opt for the portrait shape as a result of lack of recognition or just lack of thought. We are so used to reading information, we forget to make a conscious choice for the visual medium.

It is so quick and easy to copy the bar charts right out of the report or to whip the statistics straight off a page in the file. We forget that just because it looks good on paper does not mean it will make a good visual aid in its present form. We don't pause to consider the need for clarity when converting to the visual, the need to simplify and the likelihood that we'll be giving most of the audience members an unexpected eye-test if we don't! For the preparation of effective visual aids, what's easy and convenient for us doesn't count. What counts is what communicates clearly to the audience.

Shape is one thing and style is something else again, and one hardly needs mention that clean, well laid-out visual aids are going to make their point more effectively than those which are scruffy.

If you are not preparing your visual aids yourself, then you will have to brief someone else (your secretary, your assistant, a colleague or a graphics expert) to do it for you. The better your briefing, the better the result, so it's worth a moment of your time to think about what *you* want—then you have a fair chance of getting it.

Many of you will now have direct access to computer graphics and colour printers, just about the best things that have happened to visual aids since cave drawings. Yet even for these it's a help if you can develop an 'eye', the instinct for spacing, for the size of your headings, the positioning of your messages and for the dangers of wordiness.

A simple example

Let's follow the development of a simple, typewritten visual aid—its evolution and resolution. Let's say that you want a single acetate (or chart or slide), with a heading and four sub-points. The worst it will ever look might be something like this:

Good **VA** layout is important because:
- it will help the eye to see
- simplicity will make your message clear
- clarity will help the mind absorb
- colour can differentiate one message from another

This is a dreadful mess, jammed at the top, desperate for breathing space and in need of clearer thinking. Visual it is not! So you have another go, fixing a word here and there, and starting to give the layout some air to breath:

Good **VA** design is important:

- Space will help the eye to see

- Simplicity will make your message clear

- Clarity will help the mind absorb

                    and

- Colour will help differentiate one message from another.

This is slightly better, but not much. It's still long-winded, cramped and everything is equal in visual emphasis. So you try again, perhaps with this result:

GOOD VA DESIGN IS IMPORTANT & REQUIRES:

- SPACE to help the eye to see

- SIMPLE short messages

- CLARITY to help the mind absorb

  and

- COLOUR to differentiate

That's a bit better, less wordy and somewhat easier on the eye. But suddenly the light dawns! Remembering that this is a visual aid and that you will be making the entire commentary, you realise that most of the words are superfluous. All your acetate (or chart or slide) need really say is:

GOOD VA DESIGN REQUIRES:

- SPACE

  - SIMPLICITY

    - CLARITY

      - COLOUR

And you will tell your audience why this is so! Your visual aid is now crystal clear, with just four key words for your audience members to note or recall whenever they have to face the prospect of preparing visual aids themselves.

Over-stuffing visual aids with unnecessary text is probably our most common failing. Eliminating this waffle is the most important task when preparing visual aids yourself, or in briefing others to prepare visual aids for you.

When you do need the help of others, a short introduction to what you're up to and when will help to set the scene, then each aid should be briefed in as much detail as necessary, including delivery deadlines, quantities and any cost considerations which may apply.

Hints on handling visual aids

Visual aids are a prime hunting ground for that mongrel Murphy (he of 'if it can go wrong it will'), so let's run through some notions for evasive action, some do's and don'ts and some hints on handling each of the main types of visual aids you'll be likely to use.

Filled space

As we have seen, this rather oddly named category includes prepared charts, diagrams, maps or any other visuals to be physically presented, not projected. In planning these the most important thing to remember is that each must be visible from a distance—from wherever the farthest member of your audience is likely to be seated. With that in mind, these are the rules.

| DO | design for strong visual impact, eliminating all unnecessary elements. |
| DO NOT | subject your audiences to eye tests! |

| DO | prepare or brief clearly and thoroughly, and as early as possible. |
| DO NOT | leave preparation or briefing to the last moment. You cannot make last minute changes if the first time you see your visual aid is just before your presentation. |

DO number on the back in the order you intend to use. Stack neatly face down or face to wall, in reverse order. This will ensure your visual aids will be available in the correct sequence and that only the chart you are using need be visible to the audience.

DO place discarded visual aids out of sight of the audience beneath the table, face to wall or face down.

DO stand close to your visual aid and indicate each point you want the audience to consider.

DO practise until you can handle visual aids confidently and adroitly.

DO NOT play hunt-the-chart (or conduct other visual aid searches) in your presentation. This is certain to leave a lasting impression of bumbling incompetence.

DO NOT leave visual aids hanging about if you're not using them for reminder purposes. They will inevitably attract the eyes of the audience and distract their attention from what you are now saying.

DO NOT pop up your visual aid and then wander away, thus dividing your audience's attention between it and you.

DO NOT juggle and fumble and get the things upside down!

Blank space

As we have noted earlier, this category includes any blank space upon which you will create visual messages and images during your presentation. The most widely used blank space surfaces are scribble pads on easels, sheets of blank card, or wipe-clean boards including blackboards.

Using blank space is the simplest and most inexpensive way to add visual emphasis to a presentation, providing it is suitable for your subject and audience and providing you can use it with skill and confidence.

It is usually unsuitable for use with a large audience, where visibility from a distance may be a problem. Even with small audiences, it is essential to write (printing is preferable) very clearly, with strongly made letters not less than about eight centimetres deep. These hints should help to keep you out of trouble.

DO letter boldly and well, and practise until you can. (Lightly mark in lines and shapes before the presentation, if that will help you.)

DO NOT make miserable little chicken scratches that are difficult for audience members to read.

DO test your marker pens before your presentation—they have a nasty habit of drying out.

DO NOT have to search for pens that work in your presentation. You should have brought your own.

DO be brief.

DO NOT write an essay! By the time you've finished your audience will be happily talking amongst themselves.

DO use different colours for emphasis, variety, defacement or contrast.

DO NOT use only one colour. It can get visually very boring.

DO cover, flip over, wipe away or otherwise remove any message you've finished with.

DO NOT leave one message exposed while you talk about something else. It's bound to lead to confusion.

DO talk to your audience at all times.

DO NOT talk to your message. You know what it says. There's no need to keep checking that it's still there—and it's not going to go away until you make it do so!

DO use a prepared visual aid if you cannot handle blank space visual aids.

DO NOT subject your audience to the horrors of watching you struggle and fail to communicate clearly.

Acetates for overhead projection

In the raw, acetate sheets are available in clear or in a range of colours. They can be designed and projected in the portrait or landscape format. They have the advantages of low cost and quickness of preparation. There is also the possibility of building interesting visual aids by laying one sheet over another.

However, they can be tricky to handle without practice, and presenters are frequently guilty of blocking the view of one or more members of their audiences.

The most common flaws amongst presenters who use overheads are poor handling, falling for the temptation to include too much information, failure to focus the projector and failure to turn the wretched thing off when it's not in immediate use. The following hints may help you avoid most problems encountered with the use of acetates.

DO use computer graphics, if you have them. If not, have your acetate typed or prepared on new, clean sheets.

DO include a focus-test sheet, first in your stack, for use if you cannot focus the projector before your presentation.

DO mount acetates in cardboard frames, number in sequence, and interleave for easier separation.

DO decide where to put used sheets, quite separate from the ones you are about to use.

DO NOT photostat data from reports and such without considering its content, style, graphic impact and cleanliness. (Grey on grey and a smattering of dust specks is not an inspiring sight.)

DO NOT use your first presentation acetate for the focus test, thereby giving away your first message before you even get started!

DO NOT have a stack of static ridden sheets, then entertain your audience with lick-the-fingers-and-mumble as you try to separate one from another.

DO NOT discard them where you got them from, or you'll get in the most frightful mess.

`DO` pre-block any sheet on which you will be revealing progressive points.

`DO NOT` put the sheet on the projector, let the audience speed-read the lot, *then* put on the blocking paper and expect them to patiently follow your point-by-point exposé. Too late! They're way ahead of you.

`DO` use coloured marker pens to add spontaneous emphasis or defacement.

`DO NOT` be afraid to do this. You're not saving the sheets for your old age, and you can always get more copies if you need them.

`DO` decide in advance whether to present sitting or standing. If standing, remain as close to 'centre stage' as possible.

`DO NOT` block the view of the screen for *any* member of your audience, but do not move so far aside that you become only a disembodied voice. *You* are making the presentation, not the overhead.

`DO` click the projector off when you have completed a sequence of acetates, or do not need it again.

`DO NOT` turn it off between each visual aid if you are running a fast sequence. This becomes wildly distracting!

Screen slides

Thirty-five millimetres is the size most usually used for presentation slides. When well produced they have a glossy, professional look to them that can enhance presentations for audiences of all sizes. They have a more formal feel than overheads, partly because they are more remotely operated, and also because presenters cannot scribble on them to add spontaneous emphasis.

When generated from computer graphics they can be obtained quickly and relatively inexpensively. However, if produced from type and artwork they can become costly and preproduction cost estimates are recommended.

Correctly handled they are virtually fail-safe. Some presenters, however, neglect to pre-load their slides ready for immediate use.

Instead, they meander up to the machine, insert their slides every which way and seldom gain the audience's sympathy by doing so!

If you're going to make a habit of presenting with slides, the best investment you'll ever make is in your own carousel, a pack of solid blank slides and a large roll of sealing tape. Then before each presentation you can load your carousel in peace and privacy, check that each slide is correctly inserted and seal the carousel to avoid any possible catastrophe.

If that seems a bit picky, consider the fate of a Most Senior Person— who should have been more careful. Scheduled to make a dazzling presentation to a group of trainee managers, he spent hours pouring over hundreds of slides laid out on light boxes. Squinting and thinking, he carefully selected sixty-plus for his presentation and slotted them into his carousel, complete with blanks in all the places where he wanted to pause for special wisdoms.

Rehearsed and ready but arriving a bit late, he was greeted by the mother-hen Course Manager, full of fuss and fluster. 'Oh my!', cried this effusive creature. 'We must get on! I see you have slides. Good, wonderful! Let me have them and I'll put them on the projector for you.' With which he turned, tripped, and every single slide flew out of the carousel like startled quail.

Recycled from previous presentations, not one of the slides had been numbered by the Most Senior Person, and he didn't have a hope of getting them back in order. What should have been an exciting visual presentation was ruined, all for lack of sealing the carousel before he left his office. Chalk another one up for Murphy! So whenever *you* are using slides:

DO learn how to put slides in a carousel, and do this *before* your presentation.		**DO NOT** put slides in upside down and back to front, particularly in front of your audience.	
DO number your slides and seal your carousel.		**DO NOT** suffer the fate of the Most Senior Person (see above)!	
DO use blank slides to stop projection when you want to talk directly to your audience without any conflicting image.		**DO NOT** have one image on the screen when you are making a completely different point.	

DO know how to use the automatic changer.

DO NOT rely on a projectionist unless they have been well briefed and thoroughly rehearsed.

Film

There are many instances when film (and video) can show far better than you can tell.

For presentation convenience and reliability, however, it is often advisable to have your film dubbed to tape. This can be costly and time-consuming, so do be sure to check lead-times and cost if considering this.

Professional projection is essential for 35 mm or larger film and requires proper screening facilities. However, 8 mm and 16 mm can be comfortably handled in most presentation premises. A projector operator is still recommended (you have quite enough to do in your presentation), but whether you take on the task yourself or have a helper, these main points are worth watching.

DO check that the projector is in top working order.

DO NOT begin a presentation without having tested the projector. (Remember Murphy's Law!)

DO have your film checked for tears, weak splices or sprocket wear.

DO NOT attempt to project damaged film. It will only get worse.

DO run the film forward beforehand to the segment you want to show (if a segment is all you're using).

DO NOT start much earlier than you need to and then babble, 'The important bit's coming up soon . . .'

DO have the right size take-up spool.

DO NOT have to gaze in dismay as miles of film unreel around your feet. Believe it! It's happened.

Videotape

What you can achieve with videotape is limited only by lack of imagination, cost considerations, or the total lack of electricity. So unless you're as thick as two planks, an undischarged bankrupt, or are planning to make a presentation while white water rafting, you're in business.

If your office does not already have players and monitors, they can be readily hired if your presentation needs them. You can have huge screens or single monitors, even banks of monitors if it's a big presentation.

With the aid of video libraries and specialised video production units you can find-and-dub or shoot-and-show absolutely anything, from fish to fashions, aardvarks to architectural models. If you've positioned your monitors in the right places, every member of your audience will be able to see your visuals comfortably and simultaneously.

When using videotape, there are simple, commonsense rules to follow and if you are planning to work without a net (better known as a well briefed operator), then you *must* know how to work the equipment yourself—what the buttons do, which ones to push, and when.

Always check video equipment and tapes for compatibility. You're going to suffer serious loss of face and considerable inconvenience if you find that your tape won't fit the player or play on the local system. You can find that out and fix it in advance—but it's too late on the day!

Unless you have an operator, or are yourself the very model of manual dexterity, handling a quantity of tapes can be a challenge, as you thump each one in and out in turn, hoping they are in the right order. Dubbing to a single master tape, with pause spaces between each segment, will save you all this bother *and* ensure that nothing pops up when it shouldn't.

The do's and don'ts of video are simple and self-evident (*do* know the equipment, and *do not* scramble the tapes). The possibilities are so vast that you are spared a check list on this visual aid and left in peace to dream of all the marvellous things you can do for your future presentations.

Presentation services

From time to time, many of you will be making presentations in premises which provide professional conference facilities, possibly including the occasional grand hotel and lush resort. While this may make you the envy of your peers and possibly the subject of wistful comment from your loved one, the fact remains that you're not going to get much playtime until your presentation is over.

Facility managers will need to be briefed if you are using their equipment and operators. You will need to familiarise yourself with the presentation room and work out where to place the visual aids you will handle personally. If you are going to use an auto-cue, you will have to rehearse with the cue operator.

Having done so, and even if you *know* you could trust them with your first born, do not trust them entirely with your presentation! Take your own notes to the podium, just in case the cue collapses or the operator does likewise. In that unhappy but not unknown event, a pause, a quick search for the right place in your notes, and you're away again. It will be more satisfactory than having a nervous breakdown in public.

Take them with you

Here is one final hint on handling visual aids. Whether you are presenting in your own office or on the other side of the world, do not part with your visual aids. Murphy is out there waiting for them!

Do not send them by mail, by ship or by air. No matter how friendly the skies may seem, do not put your visual aids in your luggage and expect to see them again, because Murphy is a baggage handler at every known airport. Carry them with you at all times. Then if your visual aids do get lost, there's no one to blame but yourself.

So, bringing your visual aids with you, we'll now move on to inspect the tricks of the trade when it comes to the preparation of venues for your presentations.

28
Venue preparation

Your venue is your stage, and it's no use being word perfect for your part if you're going to blunder into the furniture! It's time to consider some stagecraft hints for your future presentations.

Thoughtful venue selection and preparation must become automatic for those who would become good presenters. It is nearly as important as the preparation of your presentation content.

A well-prepared venue demonstrates consideration for your audience, helps to create the atmosphere you need for your presentation and adds immeasurably to the calm, professional manner with which you will deliver your message.

The way in which you approach venue preparation will differ somewhat depending on whether you are presenting in your own business premises (the Home Game), or elsewhere (the Away Game). The development of check lists for both are strongly recommended, and the basics for these are reviewed in some detail below. However, broad easy-to-remember guidelines for each are:

The Home Game: Plan with the same attention to detail as though preparing to receive guests in your own home—for a formal dinner party, for example.

The Away Game: Approach with all the caution aroused by any sign reading: UNCHARTED MINEFIELD!

The Home Game

When preparing for a Home Game presentation it's useful to start with the premise that all things are possible, and then plan from that standpoint. If it is important for you to use *this* room but you want *that* furniture, or you want to add equipment, subdue the lighting or change the pictures—such things are usually possible amongst reasonable people, given sufficient notice.

These are the main items for which you must take the responsibility when planning and making a presentation in your own premises. You can delegate some or most of the arrangements to others, if you choose—but the ultimate success of your plans sits fairly with *you*!

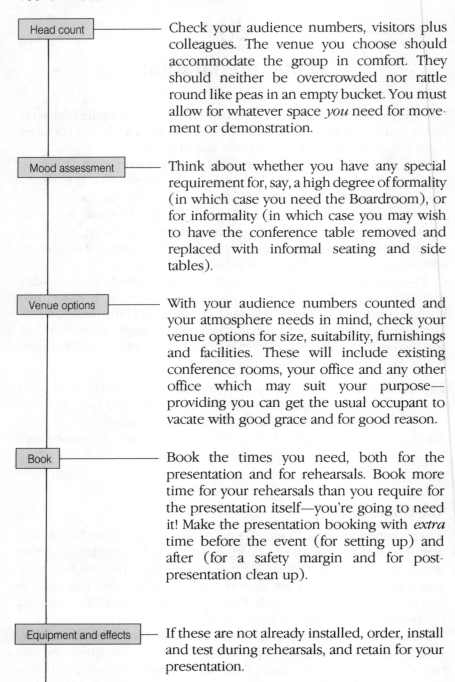

Head count ——— Check your audience numbers, visitors plus colleagues. The venue you choose should accommodate the group in comfort. They should neither be overcrowded nor rattle round like peas in an empty bucket. You must allow for whatever space *you* need for movement or demonstration.

Mood assessment ——— Think about whether you have any special requirement for, say, a high degree of formality (in which case you need the Boardroom), or for informality (in which case you may wish to have the conference table removed and replaced with informal seating and side tables).

Venue options ——— With your audience numbers counted and your atmosphere needs in mind, check your venue options for size, suitability, furnishings and facilities. These will include existing conference rooms, your office and any other office which may suit your purpose— providing you can get the usual occupant to vacate with good grace and for good reason.

Book ——— Book the times you need, both for the presentation and for rehearsals. Book more time for your rehearsals than you require for the presentation itself—you're going to need it! Make the presentation booking with *extra* time before the event (for setting up) and after (for a safety margin and for post-presentation clean up).

Equipment and effects ——— If these are not already installed, order, install and test during rehearsals, and retain for your presentation.

Seating arrangements — Plan these, if it is important to do so (and it often is). Use place names, add names to positioned agenda copies, or simply direct your guests to their seats. Remember, the natural tendency for arriving guests is to cluster together. If you want your guests to mingle with your colleagues, to fill the front seats or to leave the seats closest to the door to your helpers—or to separate notorious conversationalists—then you will have to make it happen. Be polite, but be prepared to be firm in your seating directions.

Courtesy items — Put them on your check list. Pads, pens, ashtrays, water jugs and glasses—make sure they are put in position before your presentation begins.

Refreshments — Order what you require in advance. Ensure that refreshments are served quietly, with discretion not distraction.

The telephone — Unplug it or reprogramme the telephone to your secretary to take any messages. If necessary, plan to ask your audience to mute their beepers and buzzers until the conclusion of your presentation or suggest that your audience 'check their guns' with your secretary, and promise that he or she will slip in with any urgent message received.

These are perfectly reasonable requests. If you do not deal with these noisy items you will be facing the prospect of making your presentation in an electronic toy shop!

Unclutter — Neatness counts and creates the impression of clear-minded professionalism. Have waste bins emptied before your presentation and any miscellaneous bits and pieces not required put away for the duration.

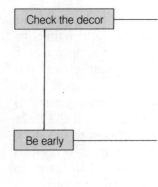

Check the decor —— Add or remove any awards, illustrations or portraits of the founders which may impress, or displease members of your audience or you. Order fresh flowers, if appropriate, but do not place these near known sufferers of hay fever!

Be early —— *Never* be on time for your own presentation. *Always* be early. Then check that all is as it should be. Get yourself settled. Take a deep breath or two. Be ready for your guests and ready to have a great time in your own presentation.

Your staff can help you

Here is a word on using your helpers. Even if your secretary or assistant is not actually attending your presentation, make sure that one or both are with you, on standby, as your guests assemble. Then if any of your audience has a request on arrival, or if stragglers need to be rounded up, your helpers can attend to these matters for you while you remain calm.

Brief your receptionist

If your guests are arriving from outside your company, if they are people who do business with you, do make sure that the receptionist has been briefed. Your receptionist needs to know who is arriving, when, why, and most of all what you want done with them. Will they be collected, directed, and if so by whom and to where? Not only is this necessary for your receptionist and courteous to your guests, but it also helps to ensure that you don't mislay any visitors on the way to the start.

Repel invaders

A final note on being early, on setting up your venue and occupying your territory in advance of the starting time of your presentation.

As we have often heard, 'nature abhores a vacuum', and there seems to be no greater attraction to the idle and the foot-loose than a lovely, empty room.

'Let's just pop in here for a moment', cry the aimless, 'for a quiet little chat'. So they do, carelessly shifting your carefully arranged furniture and littering the place with discarded memoranda. Even worse can occur.

I once took my eye off my conference room long enough to take an urgent call just before my audience guests were due to arrive. Call completed, the guests turned up and I swooped them up en route from my office to what I fondly believed was my sparkling, elegantly prepared venue.

As I swept open the rather grand double doors with a friendly 'Come this way ladies and gentlemen, please', my gaze fell upon a frightful scene.

There, in my sacred but unguarded conference room, was a crowd of infernal auditors, their paper and paraphernalia spread everywhere, plastic cups of coffee wet-ringing the glass table top, and enough scattered biscuit crumbs to feed a flock of starving pigeons! They had filled the vacuum and set up house while my back was turned!

Arms extended, in one frozen moment of horror I tried to hold back the pressing tide of visitors, at the same time laser eye-balling the auditors into oblivion. Needing no second glance, away they scurried, colliding with the incoming clients, muttering apologies in several languages, in pale pursuit of yet another refuge and leaving most of their mess behind them.

I was left with a bemused group of visitors, a conference room that looked like a bomb site, a nervous twitch of manic proportions, and the certain knowledge that Murphy had made yet another appearance. In one unguarded moment it could go wrong and did. It was all my fault for not posting a sentry!

You've been warned and may you forever be spared a close encounter of the auditor kind when playing the Home Game.

Joining the party

There is another kind of Home Game you will sometimes be called upon to play—the presentation or meeting which is already under way and which you will join only for the duration of your particular contribution. If this is a full scale, team presentation you will almost certainly have been included in rehearsals and will, therefore, know the set-up and facilities in advance.

However, if all you know is that you must make your solo presentation to, say, senior management during the progress of their meeting, you need to do some checking *before* the meeting begins.

Thus you can ensure that whatever equipment or facilities you need are available and in working order.

Whenever you are called to join either of these events, at all costs resist the nervous temptation to rush to glory, to close the door and open your mouth. Neither you nor your audience will be ready. Take a moment to get settled. Begin only when you and your audience are ready, and your presentation and your audience's attention will be all the better for it.

Venue preparation for any Home Game presentation is really a piece of cake, simply because you are at home, in familiar surroundings. The fun really starts when you have to make presentations away from your happy habitat, in alien territory. This is the Away Game, where you can get into an unholy mess if you fail to take appropriate precautions!

The Away Game

For the Away Game your check list headings will not be entirely different from the Home Game. However, there are certainly differences in detail and interpretation, and several extra items to be added if mishap is to be avoided.

Let us assume that you are planning an Away Game presentation in unfamiliar business premises, or in another department located in a building not your own. This will be your basic Away Game check list:

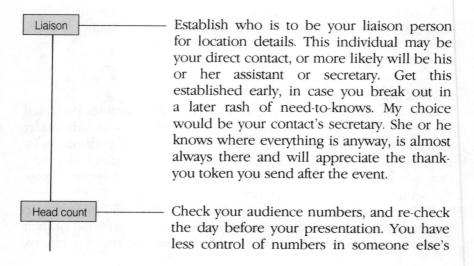

Establish who is to be your liaison person for location details. This individual may be your direct contact, or more likely will be his or her assistant or secretary. Get this established early, in case you break out in a later rash of need-to-knows. My choice would be your contact's secretary. She or he knows where everything is anyway, is almost always there and will appreciate the thank-you token you send after the event.

Check your audience numbers, and re-check the day before your presentation. You have less control of numbers in someone else's premises. Some of your anticipated audience may have been called away and others added without your knowing about it. There's not much you can do about such changes, but it's useful to know to whom you'll be presenting.

Mood assessment

Consider the options. If your numbers are small and your presentation is intimate, even personal, suggest that your host's office would be fine.

However, if numbers are going to create a crowding problem, then be sure to indicate that a conference room will be needed. Do this as far in advance of your presentation as possible, so that a room can be reserved for you.

Inspection

If necessary, arrange with your liaison person to inspect the room before your presentation. Measure it, sketch it, check the equipment, facilities and power point locations, and assess the seating. (You might want to mock-up a look-alike room for rehearsals, and you will certainly need to brief your colleagues.) Be sure to make your inspection at a time which is convenient to your host or liaison person.

Deliver equipment . . .

If required, arrange to have equipment delivered and installed before your presentation and at a convenient time. You or your delegate should be present when such goodies arrive, to minimise disturbance and to check that the delivery is correct.

. . . Or take it with you

What you can comfortably carry, take with you. If you plan to take your own projectors (or any other electronic equipment), be sure to take your own extension leads and double-adaptors. Stripping these items from your

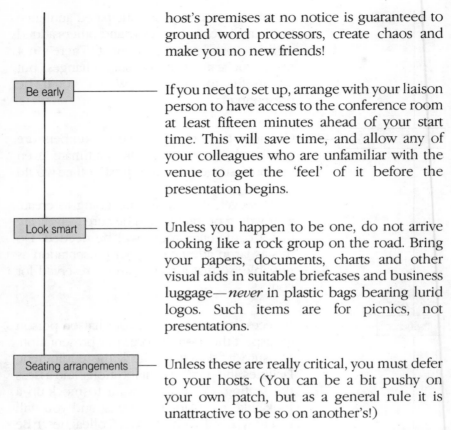

host's premises at no notice is guaranteed to ground word processors, create chaos and make you no new friends!

Be early — If you need to set up, arrange with your liaison person to have access to the conference room at least fifteen minutes ahead of your start time. This will save time, and allow any of your colleagues who are unfamiliar with the venue to get the 'feel' of it before the presentation begins.

Look smart — Unless you happen to be one, do not arrive looking like a rock group on the road. Bring your papers, documents, charts and other visual aids in suitable briefcases and business luggage—*never* in plastic bags bearing lurid logos. Such items are for picnics, not presentations.

Seating arrangements — Unless these are really critical, you must defer to your hosts. (You can be a bit pushy on your own patch, but as a general rule it is unattractive to be so on another's!)

The alternative to taking these Away Game surveys and precautions is not to think about it at all, and assume that everyone will fit and that everything will work. In that case, good luck to you—but I don't fancy your chances of making it unruffled and unscathed.

Even if you know that your host's premises have every facility you're ever likely to need, it does not follow that these will be available to you without notice. It is still eminently sensible to let them know in advance what you require. Then there will be clear understanding between both parties and a smooth path to the successful staging of your presentation.

Neutral territory

Other Away Games that may sometimes be your lot are the occasions when you are involved in presentations on neutral ground, in professional conference facilities such as hotels, motels, resorts and complexes which are set up to cater for the business and convention markets.

Passing reference to these was made in the previous chapter, with a cluster of cautions concerning briefing, inspecting and handling visual aids. To those specifics, however, should be added the general caution, assume nothing and check everything, plus the note of encouragement that these are great places in which to make presentations.

The advantages of these professional venues are the wide range of environments and services they offer, and the general helpfulness and ingenuity of their management and staff. Professional venue managers seem to be a special breed who rise majestically to challenge. Because they are in a service industry, they are backed up by basements full of goodies (furnishings, stages, rostrums, screens and forests of greenery) and battalions of muscle to move them on command. They have been known to perform miracles of transformation in the most unlikely looking spaces, and are happy to do this—once they understand exactly what you want and why.

With such thoughts in mind, when using a neutral venue, therefore, there are additional items to be woven into the check list you will develop for each presentation, and these should include:

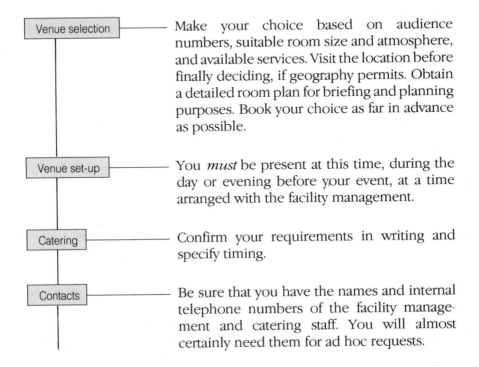

Venue selection — Make your choice based on audience numbers, suitable room size and atmosphere, and available services. Visit the location before finally deciding, if geography permits. Obtain a detailed room plan for briefing and planning purposes. Book your choice as far in advance as possible.

Venue set-up — You *must* be present at this time, during the day or evening before your event, at a time arranged with the facility management.

Catering — Confirm your requirements in writing and specify timing.

Contacts — Be sure that you have the names and internal telephone numbers of the facility management and catering staff. You will almost certainly need them for ad hoc requests.

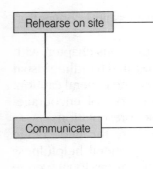

Rehearse on site —— This is essential in a venue in which the geography, facilities and staff are unfamiliar. You may know where everything is in your own premises but for a smooth performance in a strange location you'll need some practice.

Communicate —— Do not keep the secret of your location to yourself! Advise your guests and colleagues of full venue details in advance, specifying the room name or number and location in the facility. Playing hunt the presentation is no fun, and many may arrive late if direction is not provided.

Carefully covering the details of venue preparation for presentations in any location, whether Home or Away, is not unnecessary work. It's simple common sense. Your one over-riding intention in removing all distractions from the purpose of your presentation is that of achieving your Objective. Quite simply, the more comfortable your audience, the more they will be receptive to your message.

29

The final rehearsal

Previous chapters have been peppered with references to the benefits of progressive rehearsals. For learner-presenters and would-be-good performers the fact that the Final Rehearsal now enjoys this chapter of its very own should once more serve to underline the vital importance of rehearsals.

The necessity of rehearsals as antidotes to nervousness and as safeguards against flaws of content, performance and timing have been stressed repeatedly. As rehearsal motives these are all perfectly legitimate. However, they could also be viewed as essentially defensive motives, as insurance policies taken out against trouble. If so, such feelings are distinctly negative.

What we have to do is turn this defensive attitude on its ear and learn to adopt a positive approach to rehearsals, recognising that they are the source of all the improvement, all the increasing polish and professionalism which will help to distinguish every presentation you make in the future, and valuing rehearsals accordingly.

Whether you are preparing for a solo or a team presentation, your rehearsals should always be charged with positive energy and never attended with the sorrowful, drag-heeled reluctance of one compelled to attend public hangings! Reluctance and misery are highly infectious, as you well know if you have ever seen them pervading a presentation or meeting, and they will serve you and your cause no useful purpose.

It is your positive energy which will bring your presentation to life, and which, by example, will lift the spirits and performance levels of your colleagues if you are working as a team.

Of all the rehearsals you undertake on the way to your presentation, the one that really counts is the final dress rehearsal, conducted in your venue if possible, or in the closest facsimile if not.

As you walk through your final rehearsal, with your preparation paying off, with all your props and aids and documents complete and equipment checked and ready, the buzz begins. You must know that buzz for what it is. This is not the knee-knocking tremor of terminal nerves. It's true excitement. The good buzz that comes from being ready to go.

From your final rehearsal you should depart with confidence and high anticipation of the presentation itself. You may still have small changes to make before the next day, but if your preparation has been thoughtful and thorough these will only be minor now.

You may also decide to run through your notes just one more time before bed—and chances are you may not sleep too well with the excitement of your looming presentation. That's alright. One sleepless night never killed anyone and you can catch up later. The next night you can sleep the sleep of the just, when your presentation is over and the results are in.

For your dress rehearsal there are just two last hints to be added to those given in previous chapters, and both concern others—the others who will be your audience, and your colleague others when you are team-presenting.

Rehearsing for your audience

Certainly you will be rehearsing for yourself. However, in so doing it is sometimes easy to forget that you are also rehearsing for your audience and it's time once more to think carefully of these others.

For the big event at best you will have a precise seating plan and at worst a general idea of where your audience members will be located. In your dress rehearsal it is very important to double check how it's all going to look from the audience's point of view—yet another good reason to rehearse in your intended venue or its near likeness.

What you see as you rehearse is not what your audience will see, as they will be looking from the reverse angle. It's up to you to go to the back of the room, to sit in each seat you have assigned to an audience member (or in each general area), take a long, hard look and ask yourself these questions:

- Can I clearly see the presenter?
- Can I clearly see all that will be presented?
- If not, what is impeding my line of sight? Can it be adjusted, or should it be removed? Should the seating arrangements be altered?
- Does the presentation area look right? Is it well arranged, clean and uncluttered, or are there messes to be remedied?
- Are there any other visual oddities which may distract the audience? If so, what are they and what do I do about them?

Look very carefully. If you do not trust your own eyes, use the eyes of others and ask for their opinions. Between you, you will soon spot any problems, and then you can finally adjust your venue for the visual comfort of your audience.

Lastly, your sound check. This is less critical in conference rooms, unless they are very big indeed, but is important when you get into larger, more open areas. If in any doubt get a sound expert in for your rehearsal and let him or her help you. Remember, you must be audible to the people who are farthest from you and nothing is served if they cannot hear you.

It is likely that you will have considered these sight-and-sound questions of audience comfort during the development of your presentation, but it is often only at the final rehearsal that all elements together can be checked.

If you ensure that all can see and all can hear, you will be rewarded. Members of your audience who may otherwise have been fidgeting for a better view or straining to hear will be mercifully still, and yet another potential distraction will have been eliminated.

Rehearsing with colleagues

In your work-up discussions and early rehearsals you will have agreed what is to be covered by each presenter, and how the individuals ultimately perform is their own responsibility. You will do your thing and they will do theirs. However, the presentation must be linked together and flow smoothly and the method by which you change over from one presenter to the next must be decided and rehearsed in advance.

Your dress rehearsal is the ideal place to resolve this, while all the parties concerned are together just before the event.

If any of your audience do not know all or some of your presentation team, your colleagues are obviously going to have to be identified. There are several ways to do this—and a big trap to be avoided.

Handling introductions

For the introduction of the unknown there are three options, and you can employ all or some of these:

1. When sending written confirmation of your presentation you can include a summary of your co-presenters. It is simple to include or append names, titles and areas of responsibility for each, plus any relevant credentials. This will begin the process of identification.

2. If you are providing an Agenda for each audience member, you can consider adding a back-sheet which lists the presenters with the same details referred to above. Such a list will be improved by a graceful heading such as, 'Presenting to you today are:'. Notorious as we all are about forgetting names the moment they are spoken, this list can be a great help to audience members during the presentation and will provide a useful post-presentation reminder.

3. Before your presentation proper begins, take a moment during your opening remarks to introduce each co-presenter and as you do so have each stand and be recognised, if this is appropriate. Some of your colleagues will know or have just met members of your arriving audience, but this more formal introduction puts each in his or her proper business context.

The purpose of these introductions is to take yet another potential wrinkle out of the progress of your presentation, to avoid the necessity of having to do this intermittently throughout the presentation and so interrupt the flow. Getting your introductions out of the way early will allow your presentation to move continuously:

ITEM → ITEM → ITEM → ITEM → ITEM → ITEM →

Otherwise you will have:

ITEM → INTRODUCTION → ITEM → INTRODUCTION →

On and on it goes, messy, disruptive and irritating. As an example, which of us has not had to endure the discomfort of this sort of nonsense at one time or another, unctuously delivered in the middle of a presentation and oozing false delight?

And now it gives me very great pleasure indeed to introduce our friend and colleague, Charlie Farnsbarns! As some of you may know, Charlie is in charge of . . . and is responsible for . . . (this lot can sometimes seem to go on for ever!). Charlie has (usually) had many years of experience in this area, and is widely considered (by whom?) to be the top expert in his field (or, has recently joined us with these same years of experience and expertise acquired elsewhere). Charlie is a first rate thinker and

Before we go any further, I'd like to take a few moments to introduce . . .

*gifted speaker (we shall see!), and I'm sure you will be most interested
(a colossal assumption, if ever there was one) in what he has to say.*

The audience is now thoroughly distracted. Despite outwardly polite acknowledgements of Charlie and his imminent revelations, members of the audience may be silently challenging aspects of this lumpy introduction, trying to recall what they've heard about Charlie elsewhere. They are now lost in thoughts of Charlie and his track record, instead of his topic.

The perfect pass

The smoothest, most professional and most impressive hand-over from one presenter to the next takes place when absolutely nothing is said. Presenter A completes his contribution, and with at most a nod and a smile to Presenter B, steps aside and takes his seat. Presenter B simply takes up the story with a 'Now we turn to the question of . . .', or words to that effect and proceeds with the presentation.

No 'Over to you, old boy', from A. No 'Thank you A, that was excellent', chatter from B. Just a short, silent pass from one team member to the next and on with the game.

It takes considerable discipline to avoid conventional social mutterings, the verbal graffiti we are all so used to in our daily dealings. To ensure that direct hand-overs, as described, take place is going to take understanding, practice during rehearsal and alertness during the presentation itself. The team members will need to be wide awake, listening for their cues and ready to go when their moments come.

You must make your own decisions how you wish to handle introductions and hand-overs. For the smooth and businesslike conduct of a team presentation, my fervent recommendation is that you get the introductions out of the way early and get on with the action, and that you polish this aspect of your presentation in all your dress rehearsals.

Your final rehearsal complete and every last detail checked, you are now ready. After all the thought and effort you have contributed, no one can ever say you didn't pay your dues. Now there's just one more step. It's time for the Big Event.

30
The big event

Whether your presentation was prepared overnight or over weeks or months, with clear thinking and determination by now you will have:

- Defined your Objective
- Reviewed your audience
- Organised
- Planned
- Prepared
- Rehearsed
- Set up (or surveyed) your venue.

Whether you are now about to face an audience made up of people you know or those who are strangers to you, you'll be as ready for your presentation as you're ever going to get. The audience is at the door and there is nothing more you can do, now. Or is there?

Perhaps there is one final ingredient you can still consciously add to your presentation—a quality that you use every day in your personal and professional life without even thinking about it. Courage.

It's an old-fashioned word, courage, with its true value often disguised with the euphemisms guts, nerve and the rest. Whatever you call it, it is anything but an old-fashioned quality, and when you are facing a particularly important or difficult presentation, you will need as goodly a helping of courage as any fighter who ever climbed into a ring.

Consider the analogies between prize-fighters and presenters, both of whom must ultimately stand alone and do their best.

In the boxers' world frantic fans and the bellowing media applaud the champion. Seeing only the victory, at that moment the fans do not think of the deep well of courage visited repeatedly during the fighters' pain-filled weeks of training. They seldom pause to wonder at the awful raw courage needed even to climb into the ring that night and fight for livelihood, even for life, in a sport without mercy. In mindless adoration they call the victor 'Killer', and do not ask the price.

In the business world the blood-price, thankfully, is not paid—but neither is the audience in the least concerned with the drama and the details of your preparation. The seemingly nerveless skill of the accomplished presenter is not questioned. Admired perhaps, but queried hardly ever. Yet it takes barely less courage to prepare thoroughly and perform presentations persuasively, time after time—to fight not for money or fame, but for ideas.

Granted, this is courage of a somewhat different stamp from that of the prize-fighter, but making good presentations does require the same strength of purpose, determination, tenacity and the casting aside of fear—attributes which define the quality that is courage in any field and which exist within us all.

You, too, have these attributes. Knowing and believing that, all you need to do is release them like a genie from a bottle, to serve your cause when you need them, when you must face your audience with courage and conviction and see your presentation through.

Apart from the obvious physical differences, the analogy between fighter and presenter really diverges on the point of opposition.

The fighter faces an opponent, an adversary to be obliterated.

The presenter, on the other hand, is seeking unity of purpose and mutual understanding. He or she is bent on establishing a partnership of ideas, not on pummelling the audience to a pulp.

As has been said before, in making persuasive presentations there is no place for the pugnacious games of us-and-them, or for antagonistic attitudes on the part of the presenter.

So now, with attitude in place and courage in hand, finally you are ready. The hard work is all behind you.

Much earlier we likened a presentation to a gift, chosen with care, well wrapped and willingly given. Your giving is about to begin. You have every right to take real pride and pleasure in this if you have prepared well. So enjoy the moment. For this is where all your preparation has led you.

When *you* enjoy the big event, when you have done the best you can, your audience will not fail to see this. They will not fail to respond with interest and with appreciation.

Now it's up to you. And in the timeless words of the fighter's friend, 'Go get 'em, Killer!'

Presentation aftermath

31

Loose ends and opportunities

It's over!

You have now made your presentation, participated in the discussion which followed your Recommendation, Summarised the outcome and farewelled your guests with, no doubt, a heart-felt sigh of relief and a spectacular limp-fall into the nearest soft chair.

You will certainly have earned the right to relaxation, but the job's not quite done yet. So, with steely-minded determination, it's time to tie off any loose ends resulting from your presentation and to take advantage of any opportunities which opened up. The best time to do this is not two days later but *immediately*, while the presentation and its outcome are still fresh in every mind, including yours. For example:

To your audience: Confirm any decisions taken, in writing.

Confirm any follow-up meeting which may have been arranged.

Obtain and supply any additional information which may have been requested, or which it is in your interest to provide.

A simple, courteous thank-you-for-attending note will sometimes be in order.

To your colleagues: Written confirmation of decisions and summary of next actions (with due dates) if appropriate.

Verbal report or brief written summary of the outcome of your presentation to those who did not attend but who have a need to know.

Or: Be prepared to repeat your presentation to members of your company who did not attend, including details of audience reactions and decisions. This can do wonders for internal communication—and is unlikely to do your career any harm, either!

To your helpers: Your heart-felt thanks for their contribution, with as much detail of the outcome of the presentation as is right and pleasing for them to know.

Το the particularly deserving, flowers, a lunch, or some other token or memento to mark your appreciation of special effort may be called for (which you should be prepared to pay for yourself, if you must).

All of these send bright, clear messages that you know what you're doing, think enough of the project and of others to follow through, and recognise that the conclusion of your presentation is seldom an end but is usually a beginning.

Collapsing in a heap at the end of your presentation, with energy spent and freedom in sight, is quite understandable but it will not take you to the next step, the step which confirms your commitment, efficiency and good manners—and marks you as a trustworthy and admirable operator for the next time around.

32
Reviewing the presentation

A wise observer of human progress (or perhaps the occasional lack of it), once remarked that:

Those who fail to learn the lessons of history are condemned forever to repeat them.

This is the reason why you should always make it a practice to review your presentation in detail when the event is over and you have a moment to catch your breath.

Irrespective of whether you went solo or participated in a team effort, whether the outcome was successful or not, there is always a great deal to be learned from a thorough and objective review of what took place. It is from such presentation reviews that we learn how to make improvements for the future, both for ourselves and for those we may help to train.

While you are participating in presentation reviews there will be times when you will have to face self, senior and peer criticism, and you will wear the occasional hair shirt as a consequence. That is how we all learn, from our mistakes as much as from our triumphs.

Indeed, it is often true that we learn more from a blunder than from a silky-smooth success. Rather like a painful, early experience with fire, we're not likely to stick our fingers in it a second time. We have learned the hard way, that that was a silly idea, and next time we'll find another way to get warm.

When your presentation has met all its objectives, been a howling success and you are the shining hero of the hour, a review is still a very good idea. A clear view of exactly what made that presentation work so well will be immensely useful when you are preparing for the next presentation.

Whatever the outcome, your presentation review should be conducted in as orderly and constructive a manner as possible, and just as in planning the presentation itself, it is useful to make a check list for your review. It's not going to matter whether you cover the items in any particular order. They will exist only as a self-imposed discipline to ensure that you do not skip over any important issues.

For each presentation there will be specific details of the topic itself that you will probably wish to explore. In the more general sense, however, you should certainly find some or all of the following checks useful:

Review check list

- Did I/we achieve our Objective?
   (If so why? If not, why not?)
- Did the audience react as expected?
   (If not, how and why?)
- Was there a particular turning point?
   (If so, where did it occur, and why?)
- Was the Agenda relevant?
   (If not, how could it have been improved?)
- Did I/each presenter perform to expectation?
   (If not, why not? What organisation and/or performance improvements are needed?)
- What, if anything, caught me/us by surprise, and why?
   (Could I/we have anticipated this?)
- Was the presentation to time or over time?
   (If the latter, by how much and why?)
- Did all technical facilities work perfectly?
   (If not, why not?)
- What follow-up contact was required?
   (Has it been made, and by whom? If not, why not?)
- What is the next action?
   (By whom, and by when?)

And perhaps over-riding all other considerations:

- What, if anything, would I/we do differently if I/we were starting again?
- What did I/we learn from that presentation?

Not all of these enquiries need necessarily be voiced in public. What is important is that *you* ask all the questions of yourself, and answer each as openly as you possibly can.

If you were the only presenter, then your review can be conducted quite privately. However, since you were certainly not alone, the views of others should be sought—from colleagues who attended, or from members of your audience in subsequent conversations.

Team presentations are best reviewed with all the presenters present, if possible. If your presentation was successful, you may have one view of where the persuasive turning point occurred, but others may differ. Looking at the result from different angles can be most instructive.

If your team presentation did not succeed, then you all need to know why. Not in order to stick anyone's head on a pole, but in order to be clear about what needs to be done next if a salvage operation is called for, and so that everyone can take away ideas about how to do better next time.

It sometimes seems to me that those who have just completed a successful presentation float somewhere on a proud and happy cloud, perhaps for the moment akin to a warrior of ancient times returning in triumph to Rome.

They were no mugs, those Romans. To stop the warrior from getting too uppity, each triumphal chariot came equipped with a slave, whose task it was to hold the laurel above the head of the victor and repeat over and over again, 'Remember, Lord, all glory is passing!'

While it may seem a long way from the Empire's borders to the boardrooms of today, the point is still valid.

Enjoy your triumphs as they occur, by all means. But to be the best you can be, remember you will only ever be as good as your *next* presentation, not your last.

Much of what still needs to be done you can learn from thoughtful presentation reviews.

33
Encore

Now you know it all.

Now your planning, preparation and performance are instinctive, efficient, fluent and professional. 'Encore', they cry, as you make one skilful presentation after another without fear or failure, enjoying the useful purposes they serve, knowing their value to others and reaping the rewards they bring you. Oh, happy day!

For your next presentation and all the others to follow, what more can there possibly be to learn, to be watchful for?

Just two things: time and tomorrow.

Each of us has our own little herd of personal hobby horses and as the patient reader may have gathered, one of mine is time.

I often reflect that if we really gave more than passing lip service to the notion that time is money, if we really had to pay the piper out of our own pocket, we might all take a more personal and responsible attitude to this notion.

The thieves of time

Waffling presenters who fail to make their points clearly, or who run hopelessly overtime in their dissertations, steal your time as deftly as they might lift your wallet, wasting its contents like any gambler on a losing streak. Money, however, you can always replace, but time is gone forever.

In a presentation that runs only twenty minutes late, an audience of twelve will between them lose a collective *four hours* of irreplaceable time. Yet if each wore a time-cost meter and sent the presenter the overtime bill, this sloppy practice would vanish overnight.

The disorganised windbag who wastes my time does so without my permission and revokes my right to freedom because the habitual good manners of our system dictate that I can seldom simply just get up and leave an awful presentation.

I don't know about you, but there are a whole lot of things I'd much rather do than listen to a long-winded bore who didn't do any homework. Go to the pub, for instance, talk to a friend, even work if I must!

The needs of tomorrow

Now if this seems a bit tetchy, consider what happens when you tie time to tomorrow and to the inevitable development of video communications—an evolution so stunning it will stand beside the printing press for the communication advance it offers to us all.

The days of explaining your ideas to others by letter, by telephone or even in person are behind you now, if you want them to be. Today you can demonstrate an idea on videotape and a courier service will deliver it to a dozen or more destinations at once, if that is your wish.

Tomorrow you can achieve the same result only faster, with videophones bouncing information off the satellites that circle the planet.

One world is ours today, and the twenty-four hour clock is already a fact of life.

These video communications are not free, in the same way that we sometimes regard our own carelessly uncosted time as free. Real costs are involved, now and in the future.

Preparation of even the simplest videotape presentation will incur considerable out-of-pocket costs for equipment, production and distribution. The cost-per-minute of videophone transmissions will give new definition to time-is-money, and the cost of your future presentations to those who cannot attend in person will be calculated to the last cent.

The better you learn to develop and discipline your presentations today, the more you learn to value your own time and the time of others, the readier you will be for the presentation possibilities of tomorrow.

The technology of tomorrow is here today. It only remains for you to make full and profitable use of it in your bright and shining future.